CARING FOR VICTOR

A U.S. ARMY NURSE AND SADDAM HUSSEIN

BY ROBERT ELLIS
WITH MARIANNA RILEY

REEDY PRESS
St. Louis, Missouri

Reedy Press
PO Box 5131
St. Louis, MO 63139

Library of Congress Control Number: 2009933108

ISBN: 978-1-933370-92-7

The maps in this book were used with the permission of the National Geospatial-Intelligence Agency, United States Department of Defense. This product has not been approved, endorsed or otherwise authorized by the National-Geospatial Intelligence Agency, or United States Department of Defense.

Please visit our website at www.reedypress.com.

cover design by Bruce Burton

Printed in the United States of America
09 10 11 12 13   5 4 3 2 1

Contents |

Preface   vii
Introduction   A Nurse Named Alice   I

Chapter I   Sandstorm   7
Chapter 2   Meeting Saddam   19
Chapter 3   A Sad Trip Home   34
Chapter 4   Life at Camp Cropper   50
Chapter 5   Mr. Clean Feeds the Birds   68
Chapter 6   A Blackhawk for a Stomachache   81
Chapter 7   A Poem for Rita   89
Chapter 8   A Beheading on Television   96
Chapter 9   The Five of Hearts   104
Chapter 10   At the Bazaar   112
Chapter 11   The Trial Begins   122
Chapter 12   This Time It's Larry   135
Chapter 13   The Last Supper   143
Chapter 14   Checkpoint 12   151
Chapter 15   Going Home   164

Epilogue   177
Sources   179
Acknowledgments   183
Index   186

To my mother, Lola Foster, who gave me love of life and taught me life skills that still serve me today.

—Robert Ellis

To Marshall, who made it all happen.

—Marianna Riley

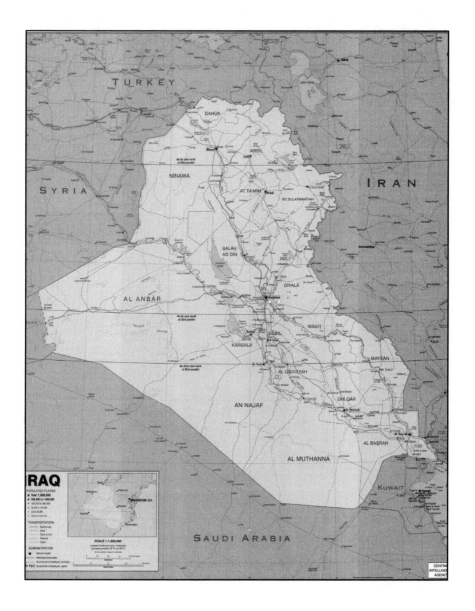

PREFACE |

I FIRST MET ROBERT ELLIS IN A COFFEE SHOP IN THE UNIVERSITY City Loop, a few miles to the west of where he grew up in St. Louis's notorious housing project known as Pruitt-Igoe. Jazz played in the background on this cold November afternoon.

Robert was shuffling through a deck of cards the existence of which many of us have forgotten: the Iraqi Most Wanted Playing Cards. The theory behind the cards, as nearly as I can tell, was to help our fighting forces learn the names, faces, and job descriptions of fifty men and two women our government wanted: to interrogate or to imprison, or both. The Deck of Cards was not new to this war— the history of such cards goes back to the Civil War when the troops were supposed to learn valuable information about the enemy, presumably entertaining themselves around the camp fire playing poker with the faces of people they might kill in battle the next day.

Robert and I were at the coffee shop to talk about his experiences taking care of Saddam Hussein, the notorious former dictator of Iraq, who was then still alive and on trial for some of his various atrocities. Robert was thinking there might be a book in his experiences. I was more than interested in what he had to say, and as a recently retired newspaper reporter, I thought I could promise, at the very least, a newspaper story.

When Robert got to the Ace of Spades, he stopped and flicked it on the table as if he were taking a trick with the ultimate trump. The Ace of Spades was of course Saddam's card, and his evil sons were the Aces of Hearts and Clubs. All the members of the former regime were represented on the cards; most were by then in custody at Camp Cropper where Robert had been stationed. "Our job was to keep all these people alive and well so they could be interrogated," Robert said. He was soft-spoken and matter of fact, and he betrayed little or no emotion.

We covered so much territory at our meeting that it took me several days to make sense of my notes. Robert talked about his training and deployment, about his initial meeting with Saddam—known by his Army code name as Victor—how Saddam had told him he had refused to align with Bin Laden, and how he had once seen Saddam cry. All this and more. Much more. Robert relayed two or three hours' worth of details, little of which hung together when I later tried to reconstruct it. Many more meetings and hours of interviews were needed before I realized both the breadth and depth of information that Robert possessed and how the experience had affected him. Each time we met, he would come up with a new and fascinating detail. When he started going through the copious notes he had taken in order to keep the kind of records the military required, even more information came spilling out.

The first question that I wanted answered—and I'm not sure was ever answered to my satisfaction—was how Saddam's presence affected Robert. Did being in the presence of the most notorious man of our times impact him in any way, or was it business as usual? Even in custody, Saddam was said to have had such a powerful and commanding presence that he could intimidate many people with a hard stare over his black eyebrows. I asked the same question of others who had worked with Robert and who might have observed the two together. None of his fellow soldiers noticed any difference in Robert's demeanor when he came from his sessions with the former dictator. He was a professional, they all concluded.

Only one other person was with Saddam routinely while Robert was administering to the former dictator's health, and that was FBI interrogator George Piro, whose present title is assistant special agent in charge at the Washington Field Office in the Counterterrorism Division. Robert and George were with Saddam each morning; Robert then made his usual rounds, while George remained for an interrogation session. (Robert most often was alone with Saddam when he made his evening rounds.)

"I can count the people who interacted with Saddam on one hand," Piro said in an interview at FBI offices in Washington, D.C. "I would be there every morning when Robert examined him— Robert and the doctor. I would serve as translator. I got to see those interactions, and clearly he liked Robert. But who doesn't?"

"It seemed to be a comfortable relationship," he went on. "Unlike most of the others who had personal dealings with Saddam, Robert was never nervous or acted differently or in any way seemed to be impacted by the fact that he was in the same room with this formerly brutal dictator."

Although Piro participated in translating and interpreting the stacks of journals that Saddam wrote while in custody, he was not at liberty to discuss much about them, except in the most hypothetical terms. "The ability to monitor someone's thoughts and perceptions is a very powerful tool as you're devising and carrying out an interrogation," is about all he would say.

He does remember that Saddam had all positive things to say about Robert, "Both in reference to the kind medical care that Robert provided and to his warm personality. He clearly liked Robert; he clearly liked us both," and he flashed an infectious smile.

The missions of the two men could not have been more different: one to break down the former dictator's defenses and pry information from him, the other to build up Saddam, both physically and mentally. Naturally they saw different sides of Saddam Hussein.

They also saw many of the same qualities. Piro said he found Saddam to be a "very likable guy with a good sense of humor. He was charming, charismatic, and friendly. At the same time, he was one of the most evil people of our modern time and probably one of the most hated men of our times."

Piro forced himself to focus on the evil. He recounted how, as he prepared for his interrogations, he would read over all the available intelligence. He would study Saddam's atrocities, never losing sight of all that was bad about the man and in doing so, he was able to do his job effectively.

So effectively that FBI Assistant Director Joe Persichini, Jr., has called George's interviews with Saddam Hussein "one of the top accomplishments of our agency in the last one hundred years." What George learned, among other things, was that indeed there were no WMD, but Saddam wasn't about to say so, the pretense being a calculated effort on his part to keep Iran at bay. In other words, to risk the wrath of (and eventual attack by) the U.S. in order to scare off Iran. Also, Piro said, Saddam was planning to reconstitute his own weapons program once the sanctions were lifted. "Until that point, his calculations were very accurate. Plus, he was definitely a risk-taker," George said.

Saddam's biography certainly chronicles a history of risk-taking, starting with a youthful assassination attempt of the then-Iraqi president and ending with the WMD-fueled, U.S.-led invasion. In between was a drawn-out war with Iran that he claimed he won, but at the cost of as many as one million lives and a staggering debt.

Piro is convinced that by keeping himself constantly sighted on Saddam's atrocities, he was able to steer a straight course and keep the former dictator from making any chink in his armor. "I never forgot what an evil man Saddam was," Piro said.

Robert's focus was on something more positive, and he extracted something much more complex—albeit more troubling—from the relationship. In knowing about the evil, yet observing another side of the former dictator, Robert, in being both a good soldier and a good nurse, experienced an internal tension that for a period took its toll.

After his return to the States, Robert hardly had time to adequately deal with all the stress that had piled on during his deployment, although he went through months of counseling as a result of Traumatic Stress Syndrome. Writing this book has provided even more opportunities for soul-searching. Knowing Robert to be an exceptionally private person, I'm sure that exposing himself so completely and making himself so vulnerable has not been easy. I guess time will tell whether it has been an effective catharsis. I hope it has been.

I also know that Robert hopes that his book will help provide a more complete picture of the former dictator of Iraq, exposing another side that is little known and certainly not talked about: Saddam's thirst for knowledge, his humor, his charisma and, yes, his humanity, all seen through Robert's unique prism. He hopes that this prism will provide another view to balance the horrors and atrocities that are an inevitable part of Saddam Hussein's legacy.

—Marianna Riley
St. Louis, Missouri
July 2009

INTRODUCTION | A NURSE NAMED ALICE

"**W**HO *IS* THIS WOMAN—THIS NURSE—NAMED ALICE? THE one that Saddam keeps writing about?"

George Piro, the FBI field agent assigned to Saddam Hussein, was chuckling about this. He and his team members had been puzzling over this very question. It seems that references to Saddam's nurse kept cropping up in the journals of the former dictator of Iraq. This was sometime in the spring of 2004 after he had been captured and taken to Camp Cropper in Baghdad.

A prolific writer, Saddam continued that practice while in captivity, but it seems that his writings weren't exactly private. In fact, his journals were read regularly, first by a linguist who transcribed the notes verbatim, then by George and his team. After that, I don't know where they went.

While Saddam was out in the rec area, someone would go to his cell and "borrow" everything he had been reading and writing, but first they took Polaroids to make sure that everything was put back exactly as it had been. During this period, they could quickly take the journals, make photocopies, and return them exactly as he had left them, supposedly leaving no trace.

I would be surprised if Saddam hadn't caught on; he was anything but dumb, and I suspect he had a seventh or eighth sense about such things. Elsewhere in this book, I will discuss how he pointed out, without ever quite saying so, that he knew his cell was bugged.

But back to Alice. George must have taken great pleasure when he realized who was, in fact, this nurse named Alice. As I later heard the story, the forehead-slapping answer was, "Alice? Alice? There's nobody here named Alice; it's *ELLIS*. Saddam's nurse is a big, black guy named *Ellis*. Master Sergeant Robert Ellis."

That would be me.

Ellis. Alice. I can understand the confusion, translating from Arabic to English. People who know the language much better than I explain that there simply aren't always parallel letters of the alphabet.

Anyway, we got a good laugh out of that. But when I thought about it, I must admit I was surprised to learn that I had made it into Saddam Hussein's journals, and I can't help but wonder what he said about me. Turnabout is fair play, I guess. However, I'm sure he wasn't planning to write a book about me, which is what I am doing about my experience with him.

Fast forward a little more than a year to sometime in the summer of 2005; I had recently returned from my tour of duty in Iraq and my belated honeymoon. I was back in my old haunts in the operating room at St. Joseph Health Center in St. Charles, a suburban community just across the Missouri River from St. Louis County. The surgeon on the case was one of my favorites to work with, Igor Brondz, an ob-gyn from Ukraine, and I was working as his assistant on that day.

I realize that most lay people probably don't want to acknowledge that anything goes on in surgery but the deepest concentration, clipped speech as in "knife, please"; "okay, forceps"; "bovie, (electrical cautery) please"; "sponge"; "retractor, thank you"; and mopping of brows. I hate to disabuse you if you're one of those, but there is often a minute or two of down time during which we chat and make small talk. There doesn't even have to be down time for us to mention the events of the day, what happened at the hockey game the night before, or indulge in occasional salacious gossip. Often, someone comes up with a good joke. Music is generally playing in the background, depending on the wishes of the surgeon. I hasten to add that we are always focused on the task at hand.

On this day, we were doing an abdominal hysterectomy, and Dr. Brondz said he'd missed me; he asked where I'd been and what I'd been doing. He knew I was in the Army Reserve, but that's about it. I said I'd been working as the senior medical advisor for the high value detention site at Camp Cropper in Baghdad. I told him we had 102 high-level terrorists and individuals, including Saddam Hussein and most of his Ba'ath Party operatives, and that my job had been to keep these people alive and healthy so they could be interrogated.

He was more than interested and said, "That's a fantastic story. It's like being in the same room with Hitler. Tell me more."

Some nice jazz was playing in the background from a now-defunct jazz station. Dr. Brondz had specifically asked the nurses to please, please play anything but country. He (and I) can't stand country/western. We both love jazz, and we agreed upon this particular station. We were nodding in time to the beat of a Boney James cut.

"Have you considered writing a book about it?" Dr. Brondz asked. I handed him a Heaney clamp and a tie on a pass, scissors, suture and waited while he sutured the area he'd just cut.

I said yes, I had thought there might be a book in all this, but I didn't really know where to start.

✻　✻　✻

DR. BRONDZ REMEMBERED OUR CONVERSATION—OR CONVERSATIONS, some as we scrubbed, some in the area outside the operating room called the "clean core," some in the locker room. After his expressed interest, along with the interest of some of the nurses, I had a sort of show and tell and brought copies of my citations and a set of the famous Iraqi Most Wanted playing cards.

Brondz later recalled our conversation: "I remember how he peeled off one card after another, saying 'I took care of him; I dealt with this one; I took care of this guy.' This was stunning to me. I started asking him questions, about the circumstances, about Saddam. Robert was very sincere and very matter of fact. He didn't talk as if this was anything out of the ordinary. I asked if Saddam ever talked about his kids or his family, and he told me about those conversations and what he knew of Saddam Hussein's family life. I asked about his health issues, and he told me about his high blood pressure. He had details about his health in his journals.

"I was fascinated. On the one hand, here was the worst tyrant of the twenty-first century, no doubt—Saddam is definitely the worst so far—and on the other hand here was this ordinary soldier, this nice guy from Missouri. Fascinating. Just fascinating. I felt this book had to be written; I was very passionate."

*　*　*

D R. BRONDZ APPARENTLY TALKED ABOUT OUR CONVERSATIONS with some of his colleagues, and within a few days, a pathologist, Dr. Marshall Poger, sought me out. He knew a newspaper reporter who might be interested in my story. Turns out she was, and what you're reading is the result.

But when I started my stint at the detention center at Camp Cropper, I certainly wasn't planning to write a book. I was too busy to even contemplate such a thing. I had to write situation reports every day and also keep notes for my meetings with higher-ups, so I had a detailed journal of my experience in Baghdad. At the first, Saddam's place of imprisonment was what turned out to be a badly kept secret. Nobody at Cropper ever used his real name, so in my writing I always referred to him in code: "Victor"—an Army code name that had already been assigned to him when I arrived on the scene—"Vic" or "My Buddy." I didn't use the code name when I spoke with him, and neither did George Piro.

After the initial interest at the hospital, I dusted off my little notebooks and started trying to make sense of it all and put it in some sort of context. Thank heaven I had kept all those notes, I say to myself daily. Without them I don't know if I could have reconstructed everything.

After Saddam's execution and a short "react" story in the *St. Louis Post-Dispatch* about me and my relationship with the former dictator, more interest rose than I could have imagined. The story wasn't even prominently displayed in the *Post*, St. Louis's daily newspaper; it ran on December 31, 2005, on the thirteenth page of the A section. Still, the reaction was pretty unbelievable to me.

I was both heartened and stunned by what seemed to be a media frenzy, as the story was syndicated and reached around the globe. Wire services called with requests for interviews, and so did the foreign press including Al Jazeera and media from Bulgaria. I heard from people as far away as Bogota, Columbia, and Istanbul, Turkey. A French journalist and cameraman came to my work to interview me, as did ABC News and a reporter for the History Channel. Although the attention became a little taxing after a while, it showed that people were fascinated and apparently eager for details about Saddam Hussein and how we interacted.

As all this was happening, I couldn't help but think about the many positive qualities I observed in Saddam and how that good could co-exist with so much evil, all within the same man. I wanted to come to grips with that.

Needless to say, I didn't have much time for all this reflection when I was in Iraq. I was too busy. If Saddam had been my only charge, things may have been different, but I had 101 other charges, many of whom were pictured in the playing cards that the U.S. military printed and distributed for identification purposes. The

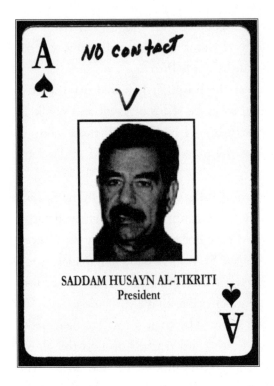

The U.S. military printed a Deck of Cards depicting the most wanted individuals in Iraq, the higher the value of the person, the better the card. Saddam was the Ace of Spades.

deck consisted of "high-value detainees," or, in military-speak, HVDs. Besides taking care of them, I first had to get a clinic up and running so we could keep these people healthy.

During my nearly year-long relationship with Saddam Hussein, I hoped that at some time in my life I would try to place my experiences in perspective. I wanted to sort out and examine my memories and observations, and then maybe put them behind me. I needed to figure out what it was about Saddam Hussein that got under my skin and why I could both dislike and like a person at the same time. I'm no psychologist and this is no psychological study. I just need to try to understand why and how he got to me.

I think the time is now.

1 | SANDSTORM

I'D NEVER BEEN IN THE DESERT BEFORE, AND THERE I WAS, PART of a convoy of thirty or forty vehicles, surrounded on all sides by shifting sand dunes that actually supported an occasional stunted tree. Standing pools of dust-covered water were on the road, which was sometimes paved, sometimes not. Squinting into the hazy glare we could barely make out the dark, slowly moving forms of a convoy approaching from the north.

Suddenly, I couldn't see a thing, as if a heavy curtain had been dropped all around our Humvee. I felt the urge to roll down the windows and reach out with my bare hands to tear away this pale brown envelope that encased us.

"So this is what a sandstorm is," I thought. It was nothing like in the movies.

It was scary. Here I was, a middle-aged army nurse from the Midwest sitting in the second vehicle of a convoy traveling from Camp Udairi in the Kuwaiti Desert to Baghdad, a distance of about 346 miles, in mid-January 2004. Then the storm hit and we were suddenly driving blind. All I could think of was "please don't hit us." And then, "please don't hit them." Never mind staying on the road.

Our experience so far seemed almost surreal and not exactly confidence inspiring. Back at Camp Udairi, my buddy, Sergeant

Major Ron Adams, had found the two trailers that we were towing. With all our equipment and personal gear, there was no way the two vehicles provided by the army would have been sufficient. Our original vehicles were soft-top Humvees, but fortunately, we were able to swap them for the hard-sided—but not armored—vehicles. Frankly, I'm not sure they provided much more protection.

The higher echelons appeared to be bewildered by our unit's inability to move ourselves to Baghdad. It was as if they didn't quite know what to do with us. Brigade headquarter's solution was to fly an advance party consisting of our commanding officer Lieutenant Colonel Wayne Sylvester, Sergeant Major Kenneth Carpenter, Major Ronald Napier, and Staff Sergeant Loren Peterson to Baghdad. The rest would have to convoy to Baghdad somehow.

But back to the trailers. As Adams remembers it, he came across two trailers that were abandoned inside the camp in the Kuwaiti

Specialist Nathan Cohen (Citrus 4), unit administrator, at left; Sergeant Jeremiah Tuzzio (Purple Heart 5), driver/ internment specialist, in the middle; and Sergeant First Class Randy Ehler (Bugman 7), environmental specialist, standing, on the convoy to Baghdad.

Sergeant Major Kenneth Carpenter, better known as True Story, and I frown for the camera.

Desert. He watched those trailers for several days, and nobody went near them. Operating on the strong belief that we needed them more than their absent owners, he made his move. It is easier to ask forgiveness than to ask permission, he reasoned. Makes sense to me. But in case the rightful owners did come looking for them, Adams had them repainted and given new ID numbers. With the urgency in getting to Baghdad, there was no time for guilt. After all, we had our orders.

So off we went. Looking back, the incident with the trailers seems almost emblematic of the way things have gone in this war, and not just for our unit. Adams called it a "come as you are war," and I'm pretty sure he coined the phrase.

Here we were, responsible for getting ourselves to the war zone, pulling trailers that we'd more or less commandeered, and riding in vehicles that were not only lacking armor but also loaded with boxes of hand grenades, flares, and ammunition.

To make up for the lack of armor, we lined the floor with sandbags and hung our flak jackets on the inside of the door. *Flak jackets* instead of armor—like that was going to help if we ran over an improvised explosive device, an IED. I was thinking, "Man, if this thing is hit, it's all over."

I soon realized that we weren't the only ones so ill-equipped. The lack of equipment was one of the major issues of this war plan. I don't want to sound bitter, but the number of lives lost because of unarmored vehicles must be staggering.

I heard about how some patriotic do-gooders back home were holding fund-raisers for the troops—bake cakes so we can buy flak jackets; buy cookies to pay for armor. We are the most powerful country in the world, and we rely on sweet little ladies to bake brownies to help buy our military equipment. I can't be the only one who finds this ludicrous.

It incensed me that our own government couldn't have done the shopping for us. I voiced my opinion about this but tried not to dwell on it. I had to concentrate on the job at hand. I later heard how some soldiers had the chance to question Defense Secretary Donald Rumsfeld about the notorious lack of equipment our troops were operating with: minor little things like a lack of body armor and the aforementioned unarmored combat vehicles that our troops were missing when they were sent to fight a war.

This confrontation came after reports were released that described how soldiers had actually gone digging through landfills for scrap metal to line their vehicles in the same way we were using our flak jackets. At least some of these guys were able to give Rumsfeld flak. (I couldn't resist that one.) Not that it came to anything. That was when he made his famous declaration that may have been helpful in bringing him down: "You go to war with the army you have. . . . They're not the army you might want or wish to have . . ."

Rumsfeld had gone on with some blather about how you can have all the armor in the world on a tank and that tank can still get blown up. I hate to have my intelligence insulted.

All this was forgotten in the sandstorm, which was certainly an equalizer, putting everyone—good guys and bad guys—at an equal disadvantage. Adams was riding shotgun on this particular adventure.

The sandstorm convoy was one of our unit's first experiences after the initial stateside training. The major who directed our training gave us Shakespeare's *Henry V* speech on St. Crispin's Day, which was maybe the first—and best—motivational speech ever: "We few, we happy few, we band of brothers." During our training, we discovered that our group was unusually cohesive.

By now, we'd given ourselves our "call signs," or handles we used for each other, especially when we were talking on the radio. Just one more little trick to try to confuse the bad guys. In this, our little band in our Humvee, were Staff Sergeant Gregory Seavey, Ghostrider 6, on my left, watching all the time for anything that might come up from his side. I watched from the right. Sergeant John Page, Java 5, had the unenviable task of driving. I, in case you are wondering, was Sleepy 8. Sergeant Major Adams—Saber 9—was riding shotgun.

Part of what scared us was that we knew there were trees, rocks, ditches, and holes out there. We just hoped we didn't hit them or the vehicle in front. We dared not slow down because the driver behind us couldn't see our brake lights. Stopping was out of the question.

Riding with no armor in a Humvee full of explosives was a little unnerving.

It was simply too dangerous. We were out in the open in hostile territory. So we kept going at sixty miles per hour.

I was amazed at the texture of the sand. It was incredibly fine. It somehow seeped through the very pores of the Humvee and into the pores of our bodies. We pulled up our "gater necks," which are mesh collars to cover your mouth and nose. Of course, after a short period your breath starts condensing and clogs up the things. We kept rotating our gater necks, and we pulled down our goggles, but it was hopeless. We were engulfed. We were blinded, and we felt like we were choking.

Mercifully, the storm was over quickly. We not only stayed on the road, but we also stayed on our side of the road, and so did the vehicles heading in the opposite direction.

When we were at a rest stop, we saw people walking outside our perimeter carrying guns. They were probably bad guys, but under the rules of engagement, you can't shoot a guy for simply having a weapon, be it gun or dirt clod. It depends on what he does with it. If a guy throws a rock, can you shoot him? No. If a guy points a gun at you, can you shoot him? Yes.

By now it was 3 a.m.; people were grabbing catnaps but nothing more. Despite my total exhaustion, I don't think I even did that. This whole experience was getting more unreal by the minute, and I kept thinking back to how I got here in the first place.

✳   ✳   ✳

"YOU'RE MAKING A MISTAKE; I'M A NURSE," I SAID TO ANYONE who would listen.

I *am* a nurse, and I was supposed to be serving in a combat support hospital unit. That was what I had done before, several times ever since I enlisted in July 1981.

In the process, I saw corners of the world that a kid from the projects of St. Louis City would never have seen. The travel sounds exotic, but we hardly journeyed in luxury, living mostly in tent cities. Still, I got a taste of life in locales like Jamaica, the Dominican Republic, Spain, and Germany. I was in charge of medical clinics in cities like Vilseck, Robin's Bay, Alto Mayor, and Heidelberg.

I actually had volunteered to go to Iraq during Desert Storm back in 1991. I was in the Reserve's 25th Mobile Army Surgical Hospital, or MASH. We were mobilized for Desert Storm, but I never left the States. After Desert Storm, the Twenty-fifth MASH was deactivated, and I joined the 301st Combat Support Hospital. I was in the 301st when I was called up for Iraqi Freedom, George W. Bush's war.

Meanwhile, on July 26, 2003, I married Rita French in Las Vegas. Rita and I had worked together at the Veterans Administration Hospital in St. Louis. She, like me, is an operating room (OR) nurse. Less than four months later—on November 10, I was called up. In retrospect, I don't know why I was so surprised. I guess I thought—or hoped—that I would not be going off to war at this stage of my life. But on the other hand, I was in the Army Reserve, and that's the whole point: to be ready. From the beginning, though, something felt wrong. When I got the call from my adjutant, she said, "You have to come down to the unit, right away."

That weekend, we had been scheduled for physical fitness tests, and those schedules were never messed with. But they had been cancelled, and a mobilization exercise had been put in its place. I knew right then and there that something was up.

We got up-to-date on all our shots, had dental work—some of my buddies had teeth pulled—and everybody made out a will. All our paperwork was checked and re-checked to make sure everything was in order. Forty-four people had been pre-selected. I was not one of them. I almost got through the weekend. But at 9 p.m. on Sunday I got a call. "Master Sergeant Ellis, there was a meeting tonight, and your name came up. I just wanted to give you a heads up," said the adjutant. I was at work at 10 a.m. the next morning when I got THE

CALL. It was some admin person. "They want you in Omaha in seventy-two hours," she said. My heart was sinking fast.

I called Rita and told her, then I went down to the unit. They were working on my orders, and I was sent to different stations to get equipment—equipment I never had been issued before; stuff I never needed because I had been running medical clinics. The supply sergeant handed me all this brand new field gear. I thought, "Field gear?" If you get field gear, ain't no place you're going but the *field*. Then he said, "Here's one more piece of equipment," and he handed me a heavy flak jacket. Flak jacket? I'm a nurse.

Then I got my orders. I was assigned to a military police company. I had no idea why, and I wasn't exactly happy. I called the people in Omaha and said I needed more time to attend to business and tie up loose ends. They gave me a day's extension.

In Omaha, I was met at the airport by two sergeants and taken to this nice little hotel. I actually had a semi-suite. I wonder to this day why I didn't call Rita and have her visit me. I guess I was just in my deployment mode and focused on that. They gave me thirty minutes to change into my uniform and then drove me to Fort Omaha. Next thing I knew, I was throwing hand grenades in full battle rattle. It was that quick.

We went from Fort Omaha to Fort Riley in Kansas to Fort Dodge in Iowa, all for different training in things like convoy operations, including what we called "drive-by" shootings, or shooting from a moving vehicle. We were taught how to break down doors and take specific positions in a house, to get as many guns inside a room as possible in order to clear out snipers. It was basically Special Weapons and Tactics (SWAT) training that lasted about two weeks.

In my reminiscing, I actually chuckled as I remembered the rifle range at Fort Dodge. It was cold and snowing lightly with an overcast sky that was darkening quickly as the day lengthened. I was attending weapons qualification training. You have to hit so many targets to qualify with your weapon, and if you had to stay out there

Proud members of the 439th: Top row from left, Yours Truly; Staff Sergeant Gregory Seavey; Sergeant Major Ron Adams, Lieutenant Colonel Wayne Sylvester, Major Mark Khulenengel, Sergeant Major Kenneth Carpenter, Sergeant First Class Randy Ehler; Front row kneeling, Specialist Nathan Cohen, Sergeant Jeremiah Tuzzio, Sergeant John Page, and Staff Sergeant Loren Peterson.

all night in order to qualify, then so be it. The problem was, they didn't give us any ammunition. We tried to tell them.

In a scene reminiscent of the Keystone Cops, someone in the range-control tower gave the command: "Ready on the left? Ready on the right?"

"No, the left is not ready."

"No, the right is not ready."

Again. "Ready on the left? Ready on the right? FIRE."

"We don't have any ammo!!!"

"You don't have any ammo?"

"NO!"

Eventually, they got us our ammo, and we started our training. It was cloudy and dusk was settling in. The three-hundred-meter targets were barely visible. There were targets behind trees, one behind a stump, and some in the bushes. It was a tough range, but it was realistic.

I somehow managed to hit my targets, just in time for night firing. For that we used illuminated bullets called tracers. If you're lucky, your night vision kicks in and you can see your target fall. We spent three days on the range, then we shipped back to Omaha to pack up and move out. Next stop Kuwait.

We arrived in Kuwait around 1 a.m. on January 17, 2004. The early morning hours curbed the much-anticipated heat, but it was still hot. We got off the plane and immediately boarded a bus to drive to Camp Udairi in the Kuwaiti Desert. The only memorable moments of this first drive through the desert were seeing oil fields and signs posted every half-mile or so along the road that said, "Another Haliburton Company." I wondered how they got over here so soon. Then, in a conversation I had with myself, I noted that they had eight months to get set up, and Mr. Cheney had plenty of advance notice.

I didn't see much rain during my deployment, but there had been heavy rain just before we arrived. The further north we traveled, the fewer the roads. In addition to worrying about holes, roadside bombs, and rocks, we were trying to avoid large-standing puddles, puddles almost the size of small ponds. Funny, the water doesn't seem to soak into this sand. It just stands on the surface, making for a muddy mess—the sort of muddy mess that can suck your boots right off.

* * *

I CAME OUT OF MY REVERIE WHEN THE TRUCK HIT A PARTICULARLY bad hole that jostled our livers good. But I was still thinking that I *am* a nurse; and for twenty years I've been serving in medical units. I could put together a hospital clinic, staff it, and run it, but lately I'd been kicking in doors, pulling "wounded" soldiers out of Humvees under "fire," and practicing on a rifle range in snow, rain, and fog— in full body armor. Fortunately, I didn't struggle during training like some of the others. I actually kept up with the younger soldiers. Chalk one up for my regular visits to the gym.

A rest stop was coming up, but first we radioed ahead to get the situation report. All clear now, but the convoy ahead of us had been hit bad. When we got to the wreckage site, we saw for ourselves the mangled vehicles from the car bombs and the scorched, bullet-riddled walls of the camp. We learned that seven people, including one woman, had died in the attack. It could have been us only too easily. We stayed at the rest stop for a couple of hours before pushing on. Grim reality set in when we learned that the convoy behind us was attacked at that same rest stop we had just come from.

When we entered Baghdad we found ourselves in a real city, teaming with people most of whom seemed to be using cell phones. We found this more than a little scary because in our training we had seen how the enemy uses cell phones as transmitters to detonate bombs. As we stopped in a safe area to unload our weapons a soldier from the signal company we'd hooked up with noticed the MP insignia on our vehicles.

"You guys are MPs . . . are you our escort?" he asked.

I said, "Hell no, we just hitched a ride so that we didn't get whacked."

Funny, we'd been in the same convoy almost from the beginning of our trip when our tiny convoy of two hitched up with the larger convoy, also headed for Baghdad. Conventional wisdom has it that the bigger the convoy, the safer. The enemy looks for soft targets. It may be only psychological, but for sure you feel safer when you are in a big convoy. Their size made us feel safer and I guess our MP insignias worked the same for them.

I'm sure this all sounds chaotic to a lay person, but it also says something about the ingenuity of the soldiers in the military and how we managed to move ourselves from Point A to Point B. Luck was on our side during that trip to Baghdad. The sand didn't get us, and neither did the bad guys. In retrospect, I was probably in as much danger on that trip as at any other time in Iraq.

I had journeyed from St. Louis to Omaha to the staging area in the Kuwaiti Desert to the convoy to Baghdad. The year 2004 was just beginning. Little did I know what surprises the year would bring; little did I know what awaited me in Baghdad.

2 | MEETING SADDAM

NEAR THE OUTSKIRTS OF BAGHDAD, OUR DUSTY CONVOY SLOWED as it approached a long chain-link fence that appeared to be surrounding a dump. It was eerily quiet, considering how close we were both to the airport and to Baghdad, the capital and largest city in Iraq. The only noise came from the helicopters that flew overhead with some frequency and the generators along the fences. It was January, and it was cold enough to need a jacket. The only vegetation we could see were some scrub bushes and a few tall trees, some of which were singed from a recent bombing.

The chain-link part ended, but the fence continued in the form of Hesco Barriers, a sand-filled wire-mesh wall used in place of sandbags. Signs in both Arabic and English warned: Do Not Enter. Deadly Force Authorized. A little unsettling, but we were in a war zone, after all. Then we made a sharp left and passed a crude guard shack. All we could see were some substantial-looking concrete buildings, one of which we later realized would serve as our living quarters for the next year. To our left, an unidentifiable rancid smell emanated from behind a concrete wall topped with barbed wire. Off to the right, we could see more Hesco Barriers. It was looking more and more ominous.

Hesco Barriers at the airport, or APOD.

This much we had been told: Our unit would be a twelve-man advisory team overseeing other units that were running a camp for prisoners of war. I didn't know the name of the camp, nor did I know who was there or why. In fact, our role at this camp was still to be determined. Originally, we were under the impression that we were in Baghdad to monitor others who were running prisons and to provide technical assistance as necessary; in the first couple of weeks, that's what we did. We went around to several prisons, serving mostly as resource people. I was astonished to learn that some jails were in residential neighborhoods. I was standing on the roof of one, looking down at a playground on one side and a girls' school on another. I asked the English-speaking Iraqi warden who was giving us a guided tour: "You guys have a problem with this?" He said, "No," but then added, "My country is in denial about a lot of things."

I also spent these first days in Baghdad going to the camp's clinic for the detainees, learning the ropes, meeting the staff, and making medication runs. I figured I'd eventually be called upon to provide technical assistance there, and I needed to see the routine. Little did I know that very soon the clinic would fall under my supervision for the next year.

The camp was a complex of separate prison buildings, three interview trailers where the prisoners were interrogated, barracks for the soldiers, administration offices, a gymnasium, and what we called the 439th Building where we held our meetings. We lived in a building that was maybe twenty yards from the sallyport, the entrance to the compound where the prisoners were kept.

Approximately ten buildings, separated by open areas we called "courtyards," housed the prisoners. These open areas were covered with gravel and enclosed by engineer tape and concertina wire. Once, there had been a few shrubs, but we cut them down after discovering the detainees were hiding contraband (pills and cigarettes but no weapons to my knowledge) in the shrubbery. Everything that pertained to the detainees, including the interrogation trailers, was inside this compound.

At the back of the compound was the solitary confinement area I later learned was called "the wood." I'll get to that shortly.

At some point, I asked the lieutenant then in charge of medical care for the detainees who—or what—was back there in the wood. The lieutenant, a physician's assistant with the 109th medical company who was showing me the ropes, said, "You don't *want* to know."

But eventually he must have realized he couldn't keep me in the dark any longer about the mysterious presence in the wood. About two weeks after I had first asked, he obviously needed to fill me in. The reasons for his change of heart are complicated, and our mission finally was becoming clear.

From my journal dated January 2004:

The 109th Medical Co. was leaving. So was the 744th MP Battalion. The lieutenant there was about to rotate out. He was showing me around and told me that the unit replacing them had no medical assets and I was the closest thing to a doctor.

I know the jargon; I know that to the Army I am an asset, just like all the rest of the soldiers—an expendable asset. In my case, I was a "medical asset."

On that day, the lieutenant said, "Come with me. I want to show you something. You may have to take care of this guy."

Very soon things started to click, and for some strange reason I was beginning to suspect what was up. First, as we headed back to the wood, I saw a sign hanging over the door to the sallyport: Camp Cropper—in memory of Staff Sergeant Kenneth Cropper. So that's where we were: Camp Cropper.

I later went online and learned that Ken Cropper had been killed in an attempted prison break by the detainees in an earlier incarnation

My first clue.

of the camp. That was before it was moved to the present site that I was told had been used by the former Iraqi Republican Guard, supposedly Iraq's crack force who took off their uniforms and ran in the face of the American invasion.

The new Camp Cropper was supposed to be a highly fortified prison where only high-value detainees, or HVDs, were kept. No common criminals here. These detainees were considered high value because of the information our government assumed they had: valuable information that made it worth our while detaining and interrogating them.

The lieutenant led me down a walkway that was probably one hundred yards long, passing three sets of buildings before we got to the wood, an area that had been partitioned with plywood. The plywood formed corridors and walls, making it impossible for those being detained to see one another. Before entering the wood, the lieutenant knocked on the door to announce the two of us, but first he gave me some advice: "Act confident," he said. "This guy is good at picking up on nonverbal cues."

All of a sudden I felt my antenna go up and my senses tingling. I took a deep breath and felt myself standing straighter, squaring my shoulders, and readying myself to confront whatever was behind this door. I think you could safely say I was "situationally aware," a term that one of our trainers back in the States liked to use. Situational awareness is something my background—my life experiences—prepared me to understand.

Guards opened the door, let us pass through, then locked it behind us. We continued down a much shorter corridor to a door that was the second from the end. Another guard opened this door, and I could see into the cell. And then I knew. "Yeah, that's it," I said to myself when I saw Saddam Hussein for the first time. By then nothing would have surprised me.

Saddam stood up when the door was opened. He was a couple inches taller than me, standing about six feet, two inches, as nearly as I could tell. He had thick dark hair with barely any gray in it and a moustache that was neatly trimmed. He was wearing dark brown sandals and what was to become his signature long white shirt, or *dishdasha*. He had been reading and kept the book in his left hand. I followed the lieutenant's lead and acted confident.

At that first meeting, I greeted Saddam in what little Arabic I knew: "As'salam Alaikoum." He returned with "Alaikoum Salam." We shook hands, and I noted his firm handshake. I checked his blood pressure, administered his evening meds, and that ended our first meeting.

People ask me if I was scared. Not really, I always say. In truth, maybe apprehensive. It never occurred to me that Saddam would— or could—do me bodily harm. But at that first meeting—and only at that first meeting—I couldn't help but wonder what I would do if he tried to escape. I stood between him and the door, and I knew that I could take him down if necessary. I also knew that there was no way he could have escaped within this fortification with all its complexity and guards. I'm sure he knew that too.

We were well into our second week in Baghdad, and now my duty was crystal clear: take care of one of the world's most heinous characters. Colonel Sylvester reminded me when Saddam Hussein had been captured while we were back in the States during our training. We laughed and wondered, what if? What if our paths crossed? What if we *saw* this guy? What if we ended up at the same place? What if he ended up in our custody? We were joking. Never in a hundred years did any of us think we would actually have any contact with the man our country had launched a war to topple. Never in a hundred years did we think we would be in charge of his care. I never even thought about it.

It is fair to say that for the rest of my deployment I was processing the fact that I was keeping alive a monster—a monster who was accused of killing hundreds of thousands of his fellow citizens, some of whom were supposedly his friends and comrades.

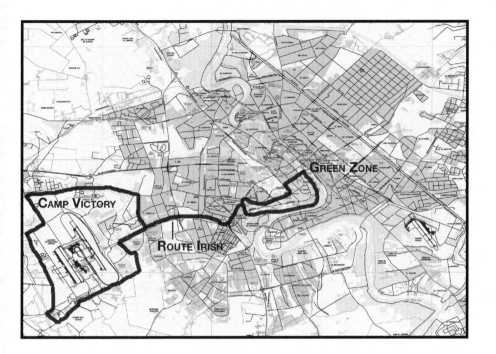

Added to this, I had a feeling that I was keeping him alive so that he could be executed. All I knew was that I was told by a colonel to keep Saddam Hussein alive *at all costs*. I will never forget those instructions. He was with our predecessors in the 112th Military Police Battalion, who were preparing to leave for Fallujah. He put both hands on my shoulders and looked me in the eyes: "Saddam Hussein cannot die in U.S. custody. That would be a huge embarrassment to the president and to the United States of America. Do whatever you have to do to keep him alive," he told me.

But I didn't have time to either get excited or reflect too much on all this. There was too much to do. I had to get this poorly equipped clinic up and running. The physician's assistant lieutenant was leaving too. Once they left, I would be it in terms of medical personnel—at least for a while.

✧ ✧ ✧

An aerial view of Camp Cropper. The detainees were housed in the low, horizontal buildings toward the top of the frame; the clinic was in the first row of those low buildings.

ALTHOUGH CAMP CROPPER WAS SPECIFICALLY FOR THE HVDs, IT was part of a much larger sprawling complex called Camp Victory. The exact dimensions are classified, but I can tell you that it encompassed several square miles and included Baghdad International Airport, which was roughly three miles from my quarters. Victory was located on the southwest edge of Baghdad.

Camp Cropper was not a pleasant place when we got there. There was a pervasive acrid smell, which was most likely burning garbage, since we soon discovered there was a dump on our western side just beyond the wall. And it was burning most of the time. It was also built on top of a landfill, and sometimes soldiers would uncover everything from vials of medicine to old dirty bandages when they started digging.

A mass burial site was to the north. Adding to the unpleasantness was the fact that raw sewage had been sprayed on a field that lay between us and the northern part of Camp Victory. To get to Camp

Victory proper, we had to drive through sometimes six inches of feces, dead animals, and dust, none of which smelled good and also must have presented a tremendous health hazard. "One time we actually thought we were sinking," Colonel Sylvester reminisced. There was a huge manhole in our compound that was filling up and actually overflowing. We never figured out the cause to the overflow, but eventually Sylvester was able to get some Iraqi contractors with vacuum trucks to pump it out. They pumped maybe twice a week for two or three months. We never knew the contents of the overflow, and we didn't care, as long as it was removed. Eventually, the problem corrected itself. We didn't know why, and again, we didn't care.

Our unit—the 439th Military Police Detachment—was twelve men strong. And I mean that "strong" part. I don't think I am alone in thinking this was an unusual group of men. We not only functioned extraordinarily well together, but also we forged some wonderful friendships. I still see many of our unit socially. On one such occasion, the colonel reminded me that the battalion we replaced had seventy-six members. We were expected to do—and we did—the same amount work. Company B of the 118th Medical Brigade from Wisconsin was also nearby. It eventually supplied us with a doctor and two medics. The 118th was also where American soldiers went for medical treatment.

More sophisticated equipment and labs for serious problems could only be found at the Combat Support Hospital, or CSH (pronounced "cash"), which was in downtown Baghdad and an unpleasant ten-mile, white-knuckle journey from Cropper. We never, ever made a trip there unless it was absolutely necessary. Still, as time went on, those trips seemed much too frequent.

The clinic I had inherited was a sorry excuse. There was a scale and a little cabinet full of a bunch of pills for everything from muscle aches to allergies. The first thing I needed was more supplies, and I immediately set to work to get necessary items, including blood pressure cuffs, stethoscopes, thermometers, EKG machines, defibrillators,

Todd Irinaga and George Piro, FBI special agents, Rapid Deployment Team.

diabetic supplies, and an intubation kit. We ordered some supplies through Medical Logistics or Med-Log, which could take up to a month to arrive in Baghdad, and often at a cross-town site.

I established phone lines and a computer so I could call people, and things suddenly got much better with the 118th so close by. One female lieutenant who made frequent visits was very instrumental in keeping us well supplied.

*   *   *

AFTER MY FIRST TRIP TO THE WOOD, I SAW SADDAM TWICE A DAY, usually at 8 a.m. and 8 p.m. For the morning visits, I was accompanied by the camp doctor and FBI Agent George Piro. After the doctor and I finished, George stayed behind in what turned out to be a successful quest for more information. The military referred to him as Saddam's "handler," but his real purpose was as an interrogator. Each detainee had a handler, and I later learned that George and his team were interrogating several other regime members. But George's efforts were mostly directed at Saddam.

For the most part, I was always alone for my evening visits. Saddam was generally healthy, although he suffered from high blood pressure, benign prostate hypertrophy, and ankle edema or swelling. We were able to discuss these things in some degree using hand gestures and relying on his understanding of English, which I was always convinced was better than he let on. In fact, it got noticeably better in a very short time.

Very quickly it became apparent that Saddam wanted more from me than pills. On one of my early visits he held up his hand to stop me when I was starting to give him his evening meds. "No," he said, and I was ready to assert my authority when he picked up a writing pad and started to read what he had written. "I know you can't understand, but I like to read this to you," he said. I think it was a poem because of the way it flowed, but it was in Arabic and I really have no way of knowing for sure.

I allowed him to continue, and he read for maybe three or four minutes. After he finished, he slapped the tablet as if satisfied.

"Now we do medicine," he said, and I took his blood pressure and gave him his pills. I think this was his little way of maintaining some semblance of being in control, and I had no problem with letting that happen. I believe in treating the whole person and not just aches and pains. In Saddam's case—in everybody's case—this includes his psychological well-being, and reading, writing, and having a teeny amount of control was part of Saddam's.

That was the beginning of our relationship. The same scenario would be repeated—with variations—in the weeks and months to come. He would read and I would sit and listen, and then he would try to explain it to me. Basically, he wanted to socialize, and we did.

My daily reports to headquarters were detailed, and I would get grief if the report was not extensive enough. I reported his weight, his food intake, how much he drank, what he drank, how much he urinated, the color of his urine, his mental state, his grooming, his hygiene—the more minutiae the better.

My day began at 5:30 or 6 a.m., and we had breakfast at 7. Then I went to the clinic, fired up the computer, and waited for the rest of the crew to show up. When the doctor and the medics from the 118th arrived, the doctor and I pulled charts and prepared for sick call. That's when we saw detainees who came to the clinic with various complaints: headaches, nausea, dizziness, rashes, itching, penile discharge, ear popping, imagined hunger, and chest pains. I had to make reports about all the sick calls we made that day. Thankfully, these reports were not as extensive as those I had to submit for Saddam.

We scheduled between ten and twenty patients a day, with time for emergencies. We also saw walk-ins, always accompanied by a guard, of course. One week, we tested everyone for TB. Nineteen tested positive, meaning they either had TB or had been exposed. We followed up with further tests; nobody that I knew about actually had contracted TB.

I would always wait until the medics were in the clinic before starting my rounds. I more or less started and ended my day with Saddam. Along with George, the doctor was with me on those morning rounds. Meanwhile, the medics were distributing the morning meds and taking complaints.

These detainees did not suffer in silence, and their medical problems said as much for the scope of their imaginations as anything else. One was sure he had some sort of problem with his toes. He had evidently convinced himself it was some kind of infection because his toes were a funny color. I figured out it was the colored lint from his socks. I also concluded that most of these guys were real wimps who had been pampered and catered to in their previous lives; some were simple thugs, no two ways about it.

When new detainees were brought to Camp Cropper, they usually came to the clinic first, where we did preliminary exams to document any pre-existing injuries. We didn't want any later complaints of abuse. In fact, we eventually started taking pictures so there would be no doubt that these guys were treated humanely when they were with us. We kept the pictures in their medical records.

Two detainees who were supposed to be so tough—one was labeled a "cutter," meaning he had performed an actual beheading—fell to the floor and wet their pants when they were brought in. "Are you gonna kill us, now?" they whimpered, in English. I just told them to get up off the floor. Those weren't my exact words, but that's the gist of what I said, in English.

Some days it was a madhouse. Besides keeping up with the regular medical exams and routine complaints, we had to deal with handlers who were constantly coming through checking the status of the detainees they were supposed to be interrogating.

The interrogation schedules also complicated our lives. Interrogators would come at all hours, sometimes in the wee hours of the morning—and I mean wee, maybe 2 a.m. That could present a real logistical headache, not so much for me as for Colonel Sylvester and the others charged with the security of the camp. If it was the middle of the night, the detainees had to be rousted out of bed, dressed, and moved to the interview site. Sometimes they were returned to their cells by sunup.

But the problem was that the whole facility had to be locked down when a detainee being questioned was moved. Colonel Sylvester said the reasoning was that the intelligence teams didn't want the other prisoners knowing who was being interviewed and for how long. Since the compound was made of several separate buildings with open courtyards between them, in daylight this could not have been accomplished. Only Saddam was kept so completely separate that no one knew when he was being interrogated. And he was not moved for such purposes.

For most interviews, the interrogators would take their charges to one of three interview trailers for interrogation. The trailers were equipped with cameras and microphones. From the main processing center, or "white trailer," you could see and listen to any of the interrogations you wanted to. All you had to do was turn on the microphones and headsets.

Several agencies were involved in the interrogations. Charles Duelfer, who headed the Iraqi Survey Group charged with verifying and locating Iraq's weapons of mass destruction, was among those who were occasionally involved in the interrogations. One time, several of us sat in on an interview being conducted by a woman agent working for Duelfer. We just wanted to make sure that things didn't get out of hand as she interviewed some of these Iraqi men who were not accustomed to dealing with women at this level. I think that was the only time I listened to any of the interrogations. I had too many other duties.

✻ ✻ ✻

I WAS JUST STARTING TO GET IN THE SWING OF THINGS AT CAMP Cropper when I got the first of what would prove to be two pieces of very bad news from home. The first was about my mother.

I hadn't told anyone at home exactly what I was doing. We weren't supposed to tell. My wife, Rita, knew where I was, but that was all. Sometimes I wish I had told my mother that I was called up. But at the time I was preparing to leave she had recently had a stroke, and I didn't want her to worry. I was heading out of town, on my way to Omaha, when I stopped to visit her one last time. And I lied to her. I told her I was going to California to help my son, Robert, who was in a crisis. All she said was, "You come home soon." I think I nodded without much conviction.

Shortly after I got to Iraq, I called Rita, and she reported that my mother was asking for me. That's natural, since I had always been available and visited her often. Soon after that conversation, Rita sent an SOS via e-mail. She said Mom was ill and wanted to see me. Before I could answer, there came another message that Mom was really ill, and I had better get in contact with the Red Cross and get myself home. But before I left, I called the hospital. When I told the nurse who answered the phone who I was, she just kept repeating, "I'm so sorry, Mr. Ellis, I'm so sorry."

I knew I would never see my mother again. Oh, how I wanted to let those dammed-up tears just flow. I kept thinking I should have called earlier. Maybe if she had heard my voice she could have held on a little longer. Maybe I could have pulled her out of it. She had always been there for me with tough but unconditional love, and now I hadn't been there for her.

I am a nurse, serving my country by taking care of a mass murderer, and I had been completely useless for my mother, whose entire life had been for me and my siblings. Now it was too late.

The Red Cross performed beautifully and got me home quickly. The trip home was grim. The only way I could bear this was to tell myself that my dear mother was finally getting a chance to rest—a well-earned rest. She had been such a hard worker all her life.

3 | A SAD TRIP HOME

I CAN'T IMAGINE HOW MUCH SAVING AND SCRIMPING IT MUST HAVE taken for my mother to get us out of Pruitt-Igoe, the notorious St. Louis public housing project and failed urban experiment where I grew up with my younger brother and four sisters. Pruitt-Igoe was horrendous and had a reputation to match. It was controversial from the get-go. Starting in 1951, tenements on the city's near north side were demolished to make way for the city's largest public housing project. It was a big deal, and then-Mayor Joseph M. Darst operated the bulldozer that began the razing in the area known as the DeSoto-Carr neighborhood. At the time, we were living nearby in a project called Carr Square Village, which is still standing.

I was two years old at the time, but as an adult, I have done a fair share of research on the development. Recently, I saw an old *St. Louis Post-Dispatch* picture that showed the eleven-story buildings towering above the surrounding slums; "bright new additions to the city's skyline," the newspaper proclaimed.

That was in 1954, shortly after the first tenants—including our family—started moving in. "The new high-rises will house 11,482 persons as compared to the 4,000 who dwelt in shabby two- and three-story row tenements that previously cluttered the site," the

34

Pruitt-Igoe, where it all began.

paper gushed. Great, I'm thinking now, with value of hindsight, almost three times as many people, now stacked on top of one another.

At first, everything seemed rosy. I went to kindergarten while living in Pruitt-Igoe, and then I went to Carr Lane Elementary School, right across the street from our apartment building. Many mothers stayed at home, and everyone seemed to look out for one another. We were anything but isolated and felt quite secure. In fact, we felt perfectly safe sleeping outside on a hot summer's night. I can remember sleeping on somebody's kitchen table down in the breezeway at ground level. The table was hard, but the cool breeze made it worth coming down from the sixth floor. And Mom knew where we were on those hot nights.

But during the days, she didn't always know where were, and we lacked the sort of supervision that kids have these days—or should have. When Mom went to work in the summertime, the streetlights were our clocks. When they went on, it was time to get home.

Pruitt-Igoe was designed by Minoru Yamasaki, a second-generation Japanese-American architect who later designed the World Trade Center and, shortly after Pruitt-Igoe was completed, St. Louis's Lambert International Airport. There are many other major buildings on his impressive resume, including two in Saudi Arabia and one in Iran.

But while his famous name provided the project with some extra cachet, he had no control over various revisions necessitated by budgetary restraints. In fact, he eventually came to regret his role in the project, saying later, "It's a job I wish I hadn't done." I find this a little sad, because he's widely quoted as saying that "the purpose of architecture is to create an atmosphere in which man can live, work, and enjoy."

The buildings had "skip-stop" elevators installed, with the rationale that they would avoid congestion. They stopped only on every third floor—first, fourth, seventh, and tenth. The idea was that residents would need to walk no more than one floor to get to their apartments. That's all fine, as long as the elevators were running. They weren't always. Many times I saw neighbors trudging as many as eleven floors, carrying groceries, babies, and bicycles.

Budgetary restraints forced several plan revisions: the original plans called for garden apartments to be combined with tall buildings and thirty units per acre instead of the eventual fifty. The revisions also eliminated the ground-level restrooms, and before long people were relieving themselves in the elevators and hallways, causing a stench that former residents remember to this day. Sometimes we would be standing in urine on the elevators. I hated that. But I'm not sure public restrooms on the ground level would have helped. Who would have maintained them? They just would have been another place for mugging and robbing.

We were among the lucky ones with a rare three-bedroom unit. Still it was crowded, with my mother in her own room, three or four sisters in the second, and my brother, Larry, and me in the third. But most of the large families were crowded into two-bedroom units.

On the floors where the elevators stopped, there were eighty-five-foot-long, south-facing galleries that were designed to be neighborhood gathering places. We used the space for everything from dodge ball, foot races, and marble games to drawing on the concrete with chalk, which, I must say, was much less satisfactory than dirt. Eventually the meetings in the galleries changed. They were gathering places for sure, but not for neighborly cookie or gossip exchanges. Gang members, or worse, loitered in the galleries and in the stairwells.

Originally, the development was planned as two sections: Pruitt (named for St. Louisan Wendell Oliver Pruitt, an African American fighter pilot in World War II) was to be for black residents, and Igoe (named for William L. Igoe, a former U.S. congressman) for whites. But objections from the NAACP and later *Brown v. Board of Education*—the 1954 Supreme Court case that ruled such segregation unconstitutional—changed this plan. Pruitt-Igoe was racially integrated, in theory at least, from the beginning. However, the policy was not reflected in reality, as white flight continued, even among the poor people. When we lived there, approximately 95 percent of the residents were black. I knew two white families, and as far as I knew, they got along with everybody just fine. They moved when it was time to go to high school.

Crime was high and killings were not unheard of, but the death rate could have been higher given the ways we kids entertained ourselves—ways that Mr. Yamasaki would never have dreamed of. In fact, I'm sure it would have made him cringe: I read recently that he was afraid of heights.

When we got bored, we would go to great lengths—vertical sometimes—to entertain ourselves. My sister Beverly and I like to reminisce about how creative we were in making use of the space available. A popular childhood game was going from building to

Posing with my sister Dorothy

building via the rooftops, jumping from one building to the next. From a height of eleven stories. Somebody would say, "Let's go on the roof and jump," and off we'd go. Just because we didn't have money for movies or other entertainment doesn't mean we weren't going to entertain ourselves. It was stupid, but we were kids.

It was easy to get there. We climbed some steps and, with a hairpin, picked the lock of the door that led to the rooftop. It is not as bad as it sounds. The way the buildings were situated—with little space between them—presented a leap of no more than four feet, and we little daredevils could negotiate the feat with ease, provided we landed just so on a narrow ledge that extended from each roof and was just wide enough for our feet. Miraculously, no one ever fell—at least no one that I knew of.

That wasn't the only way we could travel from building to

building. That was the high way. Sometimes we took the low way, down some outside steps that led to the boiler room by way of a long corridor. A partial wall that stopped maybe four feet from the ceiling, lined the corridor. We climbed the wall to get to the steam pipes that carried heat for the radiators. The pipes connected a series of buildings, and by traveling beneath the pipes we learned our way around in this underground maze. Without ever going outside, we could visit my friend Phillip Washington, for instance, in the next building down.

But we got filthy. Mom told us not to "go underground" as we called it, and one day after we had defied her she administered one of her infrequent whippings that left an impression and ended the crawls along the ductwork.

So, we invented another way to get around, this time vertically. We rode the elevators: *on the tops*, not inside. It wasn't easy, and it required a certain amount of ingenuity and daring. But, oh it was exciting, and scary at first. I remember my first time, looking up inside this dark elevator shaft, and thinking I didn't want anyone to know I was scared.

This is how it worked: Say you were on the fourth floor and the elevator arrived. You'd open the door and punch a floor beneath you but you wouldn't get on. Then, with an ingenious makeshift tool—a Popsicle stick partially wrapped with aluminum foil—the tallest among you reached up to jump the contacts, closing the circuit instead of the door. This allowed the elevator to operate with the door open and you could start it or stop it wherever you wanted. As the elevator started its descent, you removed the Popsicle stick, the elevator stopped, and you stepped on top. The door closed behind you, and your ride began. Only the taller kids could reach up to make the contact, which was at the top left corner of the door on the outside. Charles Franklin was both tall and a regular rider. Another was Melvin Rogers. Once the door closed, contact was made again and the elevator went to first, or where ever you punched. We'd punch all the floors and get a nice long ride up in the dark, mysterious elevator shaft. The Popsicle stick was a valuable tool. I carried mine in my back pocket at all times.

When it went all the way to the top, we'd hunker down to avoid getting smashed on the ceiling of the shaft, conveniently located about two feet above the top of the elevator. Once we were on the top floor, we lost control of where the elevator went. But someone invariably came along and started it up again.

There were two ways to get off. One was through a trap door from the roof of the elevator. It was best for the elevator to be empty when you made your grand entrance—it really scared people when we dropped through the ceiling. We thought it was funny.

The trap door was also the easy way. Our preferred method was to reach up and hit the lever that broke the contact points and stopped the elevator. Then we would just open the door and step off. Of course, we might be leaving someone stranded between floors, but, again, that was part of the fun.

I guess we were having too much fun to ever stop and consider that we could cause a heart attack or really screw up someone in an emergency. Once, we actually got stuck, and someone had to call the fire department to get us down. I'm sure they were surprised to see all these kids bail off the top of the elevator.

The names come back to me as I picture my old friends and remember our adventures and misadventures: the aforementioned Melvin and Charles; the Peeples brothers—Marvin, Troy, and Larry; Michael and David Downs; Ernest Williams; Hank Drew; and my brother, Larry, were all part of our roving band of buddies. My childhood friend Sharon Hall remembers these rides too. None of us knows who the creative soul was who dreamed up the Popsicle-stick-contact-jumper. According to Sharon, at least seven children, provided they were small enough, could get on for a ride.

Everyone wanted to ride. We had no fear or at least admitted to none. As we got older we realized we were taking our lives in our hands; "It could have been devastating," Sharon reminisced. She remembers one time when it *was* devastating for a little boy who fell to his death. It was in another building, and for some reason I didn't hear about it. "It was a big thing for a small child to die," she said. "I think that scared us. I think that's when we stopped."

I heard another scary story about a man who had stepped into the shaft instead of the elevator. I'm sure, in a second of carelessness, he just assumed he was stepping into a dark elevator because the lights were out, as they were frequently. Anyway, he didn't die because he caught hold of the cables and slid all the way down. Needless to say his hands were badly messed up.

My mother apparently didn't know about the elevator game or the rooftop jumping. I assume so, because we never got punished for those activities. I guess they were slightly cleaner than some of our other escapades.

Sharon and I recently relived some of our Pruitt-Igoe days at a party that Rita and my sister Dorothy Deavault had on the occasion of my fifty-ninth birthday. Sharon, who is a close friend of my sister, also keeps in close touch with a dozen of her childhood friends from Pruitt-Igoe. Most of them live within twenty minutes of one another; she and Dorothy talk daily. I think she is a good example of the wonderful friendships that were forged at Pruitt-Igoe. There is an annual reunion with a DJ who provides music for dancing, but, as Sharon points out, people don't dance much; they are too busy talking.

The network is strong, and it is active in good times and bad. If someone dies, or someone's mother or husband dies, the Pruitt-Igoe friends will be there. They will come and they will sit with the bereaved. I don't remember much, but when Mama died, maybe three dozen people from Pruitt-Igoe came with condolences—friends of ours and friends of hers, of whom there were many.

In the 1960s, thanks in part to the prevailing drug culture, life in the projects changed. Where once people felt secure and close and neighbor looked after neighbor, we now lived in a constant state of fright. And not just at night. We heard gunshots that were too close for comfort. Both my mother and I were robbed at gunpoint.

Fights were common and so were robberies. If you were robbed, there was a good chance that it was by someone you knew. We never went to the authorities. We just tried to handle all the problems ourselves. We started getting guns and knives—arming ourselves— for our own defense. I knew people who stole guns for this purpose. Many of us had knives: yellow-handled Case knives with three X's etched on the blade. We'd oil them and then work them back and forth until we could pop 'em as fast as a switchblade. Then we would slit a hole in the flap that covers the zipper in our pants and that's where we carried it, in case we were stopped and frisked by the police.

Self protection. It was something we learned early; it was all part of living there. I'm sure it's not much different in any hostile environment, part of everyday living in places like Cabrini Green in Chicago, Five Points in nineteenth-century New York, the slums of Mumbai, or even certain remote villages in Iraq for that matter. If we were robbed, we were usually told, "Better not tell anybody." Of course we told people, and if you ran into that person again you might crack his head.

When I was ten or eleven, I was a paperboy. It seems so quaint now, but on weekends people would hang out their windows and yell down for a paper. I carried a specified number of papers that I had picked up at the "paper branch" on Jefferson about a half block south of Easton Avenue (now Martin Luther King). I'd respond, "What apartment are you in?" and once I got the number, I'd head up. We had to take our wagons with us because if we didn't, when we came back they would be gone. I was fortunate; I never got robbed of my money and papers. Some friends of mine did. The bad guys took their money and papers, and then they threw the empty wagon at them.

A short piece in a local paper in 1969 said that firefighters were threatening to refuse to respond to fires in Pruitt-Igoe without adequate police protection. Firefighters were reported dodging everything from bullets to rolling pins to wringers from washing machines that were hurled at them. I have reason to think that police protection, too, was scarce, because of the danger to the officers.

I made myself a promise that when I got out I'd never live in public housing again. And I didn't.

My poor long-suffering mother. When I think now, as an adult, of all that Lola Foster had to contend with, I'm in awe.

She might as well have been single, because we never saw a penny of the money my father made working on the assembly line at the local General Motors plant. In fact, we almost never saw him. I guess he visited a few times in order to make all those babies.

Lola Foster was a hustler, and I mean that in the best sense. She went to work every day—conducting vision tests for the Missouri Department of Motor Vehicles and working as a domestic—and we kids looked after each other. We had chores to do, and there would be hell to pay if we didn't do them. Between Mom's scrimping and all the Eagle Stamps we licked, she was always able to get us Christmas presents. But I think I was in my teens before I ever tasted any part of the chicken besides the neck and the back.

By 1968, when I was still a teenager, she miraculously had saved enough money to buy a small two-family flat with four or five rooms on each floor. It was slightly more than two miles from Pruitt-Igoe, where by then we had lived for fourteen years, but it seemed a world away. We thought we had gone to heaven.

Shortly after we left, the St. Louis Housing Authority vacated most of the buildings; by 1972 the authority had razed three of the buildings, and by 1976 the entire complex was dynamited. It was a failure noted by urban planners and architects alike, seen as one more example of the inadequacy of government in solving social problems as well as a failure of architecture. But we were safely away

Mom

by that point, and although we undoubtedly saw the lingering cloud of dust when the buildings went down, I watched the implosion on TV. Looking back from a post-9/11 perspective, I can't help but see some irony in how the much-published picture of Mr. Yamasaki's Pruitt-Igoe buildings toppling has now been supplanted by the iconic image of the World Trade Center collapsing.

But those images weren't part of our world and neither were the laments of the urban planners and the architects and the sociologists. We were outta there. With twice as much space, we now had carpeted floors instead of the concrete in the projects. There was a little stained glass window in the door and a small chandelier in the living room. The two apartments had already been connected with interior stairs so we could go from one story to the other without going outside. We had a fenced-in backyard and a garage that stood empty because we didn't even have any bicycles to put there, much less a car. Eventually when I was nineteen, I bought my first car. I paid $150 for a 1948 Buick Roadmaster that was older than me.

We loved living there at West Florissant and College avenues in north St. Louis. The houses around us were so pretty and neat, and all the people kept up their property. However, within about a year of our move, we could see that this neighborhood, too, was starting to change, for the worse.

It would be a long climb to the middle-class life I am leading now.

*   *   *

I GOT HOME FOR THE FUNERAL WITHIN TWO DAYS. ALL MY SIBLINGS were already gathered except for the oldest, Norma. We had lost her the year before to cervical cancer. Somehow she had managed to keep us in the dark about it until almost the very end.

Besides the Pruitt-Igoe friends, some of my Army buddies from the deactivated 25th MASH and the 301st CSH were there to show their support. My nieces and nephews were there too. They all had been very close to my mother and were deeply upset, so distraught, in fact, that I felt I couldn't let my own grief show. I had to be strong for them.

After a few days at home, I felt myself going into a downward spiral. I was having a hard time accepting my mother's death. I felt overwhelming sadness, along with extreme fatigue. But I couldn't sleep, and I had trouble concentrating on even the simplest tasks. For some reason I also felt a horrendous guilt, which hardly seemed appropriate, considering everything. I don't think I ever had been depressed before, but I could feel it coming on. The day of the funeral was especially bad for me.

Although I could have stayed at home longer, it seemed pointless. The longer I hung around, the worse these symptoms became. This was definitely a low point in my life.

I thought I needed work to take my mind off my grief, and after about a week, I started making phone calls to see when I could get the next flight to Baghdad. On the return trip to Baghdad I tried to sleep, but my own reality kept interfering. Although I didn't want to be in St. Louis, I wasn't sure I was ready to face what I was up against at Camp Cropper, especially Saddam Hussein.

Maybe it was part of the grieving process, but I was bitter and angry and in real need of kicking something. Here we were, working day and night to keep alive these assholes who had committed so many atrocities, when I was needed in St. Louis to take care of my own family. I had a new wife, a brother who wasn't in the best of health, and a mother who might have been helped if I had been there. Duty is a harsh taskmaster for sure.

I thought about Saddam and how courteous and compliant he had been. I wondered how he felt about me—if he included me in the hatred he was known to have for everything American. I wondered whether he was using me, or if he planned to. Could that happen even without my knowledge? I remembered reading about how a guard at the Nuremberg trials unknowingly carried a cyanide pill to Hermann Goering so he could escape a hanging. Did Saddam have similar designs?

Watch your back, Ellis, I told myself. Be on guard. Watch every move, and don't let him get to you. I wasn't exactly afraid for my physical self, but something I couldn't identify was making me anxious. I think this guy was starting to get under my skin, but I wasn't sure why.

I finally fell into an uneasy sleep.

* * *

W HEN I RETURNED TO CAMP CROPPER, MY "COMPLIANT" CHARGE was on a hunger strike. I went to see him that night; the guards had already reported he hadn't eaten for maybe three days.

"They tell me you're not eating," I said. You don't like the food?"

He replied, "No, no objection to food."

"Then why don't you eat?"

He shrugged his shoulders and raised his hands. "No objection to food. Object to being fed through a slot. Like a lion." (I noticed that he could speak almost perfect English when he wanted to.) At that time, the detainees were given MREs (meals ready to eat), the same as we ate. The procedure was to open them, take out anything that could possibly be used as a weapon, then open the hatch that was on every door, and set the tray inside.

Although he was drinking water, I felt I could see him shrinking before my very eyes. I checked on him every couple of hours. He continued to go to the recreation area, but he was dizzy and wobbly. I gave him two Tylenol for a headache that he admitted he had, but he still refused to eat.

"I will go out and talk with my commander and see what I can do," I told him.

It was Colonel Sylvester's turn. He recently recalled putting on all his body armor, helmet, and pistol for this encounter—anything to look as official as possible. "I hear you don't like the program around here," he said to Saddam.

Saddam repeated, "I object to the way I'm fed. I'm a man, not an animal." The colonel hung tough. These are the rules of the camp. These are our feeding procedures, he said, and you, Saddam, are being treated the same as everyone else. End of conversation.

We seemed stalemated.

Eventually, I decided enough was enough. "The powers that be don't really care if you eat or not, but they're not going to let you die in here," I told him. "If necessary they can strap you down and feed you with an IV or whatever it takes."

I thought maybe what I said had some effect because at 8:10 p.m. that same day I reported:

Ate small amount of food from dinner tray. Took evening meds with water; appeared to be in good spirits and stated that his head felt heavy but no pain.

I later learned that some other forces had been at work and that I couldn't claim any credit for ending the hunger strike.

George Piro was a key player in the return of Saddam's appetite, and I later discovered that a resolution to the hunger strike was essential for George's purposes. He saw Saddam's hunger strike as a power struggle, pure and simple. It began, George said, as he was beginning to make significant gains in his interrogation. Saddam sensed that, George said. "Absolutely. We could see it in his demeanor, his responses, his reactions to the questions. We were clearly making good progress," he said. "It was critical for us to get him over it without really giving in. We had to stand firm. And we did. Giving in would have negatively impacted our interrogation plan . . . we had to convince him to eat."

Colonel Sylvester was also in on the plan. He was helping George build a bond with Saddam while creating the impression that he, George, had influence and control.

On the third day, the guards reported that Saddam, on his latrine break, had tried to sneak some food from the trays that had been left—conveniently, I'm thinking now—right outside his door.

About this time, there was a change of the guard. A new unit was coming in, and somehow everybody got it quietly worked out that Saddam could carry in his own tray. George acquired a new aura of power, the colonel still had given the appearance of reading the riot act, and Saddam started eating again. He'd gone without food for about five days. Saddam later told George that he started eating again because of him. "He said he did it just for me," George said.

George now says that the hunger strike was a major turning point in his interrogations. Why? "Because I won," he said with a laugh. "And he knew it."

It didn't happen all at once, and he resumed eating slowly. The day after my conversation with him, he ate a pancake and drank a half-pint carton of grape juice. The dizziness continued for a few more days.

I also meant what I said. If necessary we could have force-fed the old boy. I'm glad it didn't come to that.

The hunger-strike episode was my first major encounter with Saddam's will, and I was satisfied with the result. I felt as if everyone involved had been rational and that maybe Saddam had reacted to reason. I felt that we had made some compromises as well. Let's hear it for Conflict Resolution 101.

4 | LIFE AT
CAMP CROPPER

ALTHOUGH HIS HUNGER STRIKE WAS OVER, VIC CONTINUED TO lose weight. When he had lost about 11 pounds and reached 169 pounds, he said this was the weight where he felt best. The higher-ups weren't happy and told us to get his weight back up. They wanted him looking healthy and fat, like us. So I started taking him extra snacks, but I felt like I was fattening him up for the kill. It was bothering me increasingly, and I seemed to be asking myself more and more often, why were we bothering?

There was something wrong with this picture, and although I was a small cog, I nevertheless was part of it. We set him up; he killed maybe hundreds of thousands of people in a regime we then decided was immoral; we launched a war to stop him and lost a few thousand of our own people in the process; we captured him and treated him humanely and sensitively; we kept his blood pressure in check and treated his small ailments; then eventually we would give him back to the Iraqis who would execute him.

And I'm aiding and abetting because I'm a good soldier.

As to the problem of the extra food, Saddam gave most of the snacks away. "I eat enough for my activity level—what am I doing here?" he asked rhetorically. In fact, all he did was read and pray and walk outside a couple times a day. The nurse in me agreed completely. This guy has some good instincts.

In general, the nurse in me felt good about what we were able to do for all the detainees, not just Saddam Hussein. In the beginning, we suffered mightily for lack of supplies and equipment. Our medical facility, however, became a lot more efficient after a significant, but unfortunate, event that resulted in the death of one of our most infamous detainees, Muhammed Abu Abbas.

You may remember him. He was not in the Deck of Cards, nor did he have much to do with the reason we were in Iraq in the first place, but he was caught in the same snare that netted other higher value detainees.

Even more than twenty years after it happened, he is remembered as the mastermind of the hijacking of the *Achille Lauro*, an Italian cruise ship on which an American Jew, Leon Klinghoffer, was shot then dumped into the Mediterranean Sea. He was still seated in his wheelchair as he was thrown overboard.

In October 1985, an outraged world watched news reports of this hijacking; I was among them. I read later that Abbas denied planning to kill anyone, that the killing was part of a botched plan.

Then, for a time, he was a Palestinian hero—his title was the general director of the Palestine Liberation Front—a U.S. government–designated terrorist organization—supposedly advising certain Middle Eastern countries and the Palestinian National Authority on reaching a lasting peace. At one point, then-President George W. Bush accused Saddam of harboring Abbas, who was captured by U.S. Special Forces in the outskirts of Baghdad.

A big man, at least six feet tall and easily over two hundred pounds, he was known to be able to keep control in the large group cell he shared with maybe a dozen other detainees. The few times I had seen him before, he seemed to always have his hand out, presumably collecting some sort of protection dues from the other detainees. At least that's one theory. Why they would need protection is beyond me. But all I know is that I heard him asking for "weight." At least that's what it sounded like.

So here he was in U.S. custody as our responsibility. He was the reason I was roused from a deep sleep as someone pounded on my door in the early morning hours on March 8. "We got a flatliner in the clinic," said the sergeant who was doing the pounding. "Flatline" means the EKG shows no cardiac activity, not the usual peaks and valleys. Not a good sign. I tore down there to find No. 39 (Abbas) lying on a stretcher. I was a little surprised, because he seemed to be one of the healthy ones, not even on the medication schedule. He had never come to "sick call." Turns out, the first time he was in the clinic he was having a heart attack.

This guy was in cardiac arrest then. I found out later that he had complained of chest pains to the guards who offered him a ride on a stretcher, but he insisted on walking to the clinic, a distance of about fifty feet from his cell. Then he got up on the stretcher by himself in what was his last act. By this time, a doctor then assigned to Camp Cropper was there, along with two medics from the 118th. The doctor had already run to get the defibrillator that we kept in the room next to Saddam. Then we shocked Abbas and placed an ambu bag over his nose and mouth in an attempt to ventilate him.

I immediately joined in the CPR effort. We also tried to establish an airway, although we couldn't intubate him because we didn't have the proper equipment. Abbas had a very fat neck and, try as hard as we did repositioning his head, we couldn't get his airway open. I could tell the air was not getting into his lungs but rather going into his abdomen. In fact, I could hear the air swishing down there, which meant we weren't getting a tight seal around his nose and mouth. Obviously, we weren't being very effective.

I took over the compressions, but I saw him turning blue and I knew we were losing him. Having a patient slip away while in your grasp is one of the most helpless feelings a medical professional can experience. You are doing everything you know to save a person, and it's just not happening. We knew that Abbas was a terrorist, but that was all forgotten as we tried to save his life. I think I would not have tried harder for my own mother.

By now, the Air Force had been notified because they could get a patient in deep distress to the Combat Support Hospital faster than we could; they would go first by ambulance to their clinic at the APOD (Aerial Port of Debarkation, shortened for obvious reasons; lay folks would just say "airport"). The Air Force crew took over when they got there, and we assisted with CPR en route to the ambulance; I'm sure they pronounced him dead as soon as they got him to their clinic.

Looking back, we gave it our best shot considering what we had to work with. Despite our hard work in putting together the clinic, I clearly saw our deficiencies in both equipment and clinical skills. First, the doctor was a gynecologist, who probably hadn't run a code since he was a resident. Although he appeared to be in good shape, he worried me a little with his huffing and puffing after running down to the wood to get Saddam's defibrillator.

After we lost Abbas, there was an investigation and all of a sudden we got some attention. I saw more generals on this tour than I have seen in my entire military career, and they all wanted to know what we needed to keep this from happening again. Suddenly, we had many more channels through which we could get all the equipment and supplies necessary to support an acute care facility. First of all, we got a laryngoscope, an instrument that is used to open the airway so that a breathing tube can be inserted. We got other things as well: portable oxygen tanks, a portable defibrillator, an otoscope, a computer and printer, and all kind of brand-name medicines.

One of the first things we did when we started getting the supplies was put together a trauma bag that contained bandages, local anesthetics, stethoscope, blood pressure cuff, alcohol wipes, IV needles, tubing, bags of normal saline, sterile water, thermometers, a small oxygen tank, and other items that we might need in an emergency. It was kept in the clinic near the front door. We hardly ever used it, but I felt it was good insurance.

Eventually, I got a phone installed in the doc's room, which helped cut our response time considerably, eliminating the time for someone to run to the next building and pound on the doc's door.

In addition to getting more equipment, we also changed our *modus operandi*. For one thing, we started seeing all detainees in the clinic once a month, regardless of whether they had actual complaints and regardless of whether they wanted the checkup.

Clearly our government didn't want us to lose any more HVDs, who were needed for interrogation purposes. And we didn't. I'm proud of our track record. I got a new doctor and two medics every ninety days, so I had to train a new crew every three months. I felt the high standards of care remained the same because of a good program that we didn't deviate from.

Ours was a far cry from the clinic I inherited and an even farther cry from the first Camp Cropper that some people called America's Gulag. I never saw it, but I admit it sounded horrendous. Prisoners were housed in a tent city out in the desert with barely enough water to drink, much less bathe in. In reality, it was maybe a couple hundred yards from where we were, but the difference seems more like light years. The military shut down the first Camp Cropper in October, a few months before I got there, and they moved the HVDs—the ones wanted for interrogation—to the "new" facility, the barracks where we were now staying.

So we lucked out. The buildings were substantial, making us feel a lot safer. The reinforced concrete that these barracks were constructed with meant they would probably survive a rocket or mortar attack. I'm sure that's why the military kept those buildings, and as long as the HVDs were safe, by extension so were we. At least that's what we told ourselves.

Between the upgraded equipment and relatively safe living conditions, our charges got better care than many people back in the

States. These guys got top-of-the-line medicines, and our response time was four minutes max from the time a call went out until we showed up. That's from being awakened from a sound sleep, getting dressed, and running to the clinic.

We also gave priority to chest pains after Abu Abbas. Some of the detainees figured that out and probably took advantage, sometimes getting a trip to the CSH for evaluation in the bargain. They seemed to like the idea, even though they were blindfolded and shackled for the entire trip, which was often very dangerous for all of us. I guess any diversion to get them out of camp would do, but that's another story.

My commanding officer, Jayhawker 6—or Colonel Sylvester—made the point that one of the major challenges of this mission was the "non-doctrinal" nature of it. Army doctrine doesn't cover what to do with former regime members when you invade a country. There are doctrines that discuss military personnel and civilian returnees, but how the former political heads of a country are handled is a bit of a gray area, according to Sylvester. Army doctrine allows for work details for prisoners of war, for instance, but not what to do with a guy with hypertension or a fifty-five year old with diabetes.

In essence we were making up the rules as we went along, and it was sometimes chaotic. I remember when Colonel Sylvester asked the higher-ups for guidance. They said, "Just run it." They didn't care about shortages of supplies, equipment, or men. The word was "just get it done." Sylvester laughed, "I don't know if they just trusted us or wanted all this to be out their hair." Also, Sylvester pointed out, as the mission progressed we became the facility of choice to hold high-level insurgent leaders or people who posed a unique security threat to the new Iraqi government.

A further problem, especially for me, was the multitude of ailments our charges had and the chronic nature of these ailments. The ages of our detainees ranged between forty and seventy, but most were on the far side of middle age, so much so that at one point the average age was around sixty. That lowered somewhat over time.

The point is that many of their medical conditions were in great part a function of age including, but not limited to, tuberculosis exposure, diabetes, glaucoma, arthritis, hypertension, heart disease—just about any geriatric disease you can name, one of our charges had it.

Some of these guys were real pains in the ass. Vic might have been the Ace of Spades and by far the highest profile detainee, but he certainly wasn't the highest maintenance. That was fortunate, because I had 101 other HVDs in my care and the clinic to run. Saddam didn't complain much, and when he did it was legitimate. If all the detainees were like Saddam it would have been an easy tour for me. If he complained, it was usually legit—no whining or bawling from him. I guess prison was a shock to these guys, who previously had everything they wanted with a finger snap.

The second-highest profile, as his rank in the Most Wanted Deck indicates, was Chemical Ali. The King of Spades, former Ba'athist Iraqi defense minister, interior minister, military commander and chief of the Iraqi Intelligence Service, presidential advisor, member of the Revolutionary Command Council, and governor of occupied Kuwait during the Gulf War, Ali Hassan al-Majid was definitely part of Saddam's inner circle. Like Saddam, he didn't complain much, but he was high maintenance for other reasons, mostly related to his health problems. He was Saddam's cousin, who at sixty-three walked with a cane and looked considerably older than his infamous cousin. In fact, he was four years younger. He had insulin-dependent diabetes and took regular injections. He also loved chocolate.

Chemical Ali was the name given him by a) the U.S. b) Iran c) the Kurds, depending on your sources. Certainly, the name fit in well with U.S. propaganda, as Chemical Ali was accused of issuing the order to gas the Kurds. I have since read some compelling material to the effect that the evidence is slim that it was actually Ali Hassan al-Majid who ordered a poison-gas attack against the residents of

Chemical Ali

Halabja, where thousands of civilians were, indeed, killed. It was after this incident that he earned his nickname, and, in fact, this incident was one of the reasons our government used for the Iraq invasion.

A *New York Times* story on January 31, 2003, claims that indeed there were many casualties of a gas attack in Halabja during the Iran-Iraq War, but that's what they were: casualties of war. According to this account, both sides used gas, but the civilians were not the primary target and an analysis of the dead Kurds' bodies suggested they had been killed with a cyanide-based gas, which Iran was known to use. Iraqis were thought to have used mustard gas in the battle and didn't have blood agents such as cyanide at the time. But Halabja was only one of several villages where Kurds were gassed and, despite the *New York Times* story, there is evidence that Chemical Ali was out to get the Kurds and other dissidents in whatever way possible. It is also probably safe to say that Chemical Ali deserves whatever he gets, which at my last count was three separate death sentences plus numerous prison terms for other inhumane acts. He, apparently, remained unapologetic, saying it was all done to quell rebellion.

Deserving of punishment as I knew Chemical Ali was, still I grew cynical about government information, considering the primary justification for invading Iraq—WMD—proved false. If this was based on faulty intelligence—as I believe it was—could not other information we have been given also be wrong or misleading?

Chemical Ali was frail. He went into insulin shock on at least two different occasions when he was under our care. At least one of these incidents took place during Ramadan. Frankly, I don't think a diabetic should be fasting, but he didn't ask me. In fact, he told me he could manage his diabetes and had been doing so very well over the year, giving himself insulin shots at least twice a day.

Ron Adams, who had day-to-day operational control of everything that went on in the prison, recently told me that before he left Iraq he got a letter from al-Majid thanking him for taking care of him. The letter also contained a not-unreasonable request.

Here's the translated version of the letter, courtesy of Ron Adams:

> *In the name of God the merciful and compassionate,*
> *Mr. Adams, the administrative director.*
> *I greet you with Islam greeting and say peace upon you, and God's blessings.*
> *I ask you to agree to return my black sweater from my colleague (Nasim) down the block, #5 I think his room # is 5 and his # is 111. I also ask you to provide me with winter jacket.*
> *I seize this opportunity to thank you for taking care of us all. May God grant you and your family success.*
> *detainee #125*
> *Ali Hassan Al Majid*

"He was happy to be with us, because every day he was with us was one more day he was alive," Adams said.

The last I heard was that Chemical Ali was still alive, which surprises me. He was sentenced to death in 2007 and another death sentence was imposed late last year and another in March 2009. The most recent was for the 1999 killing of Shia Muslims in Baghdad's Sadr City area and also the city of Najaf. His executions have been delayed by legal wrangling and, as we go to press, the execution has not occurred.

At the other end of the spectrum, Saddam's half-brother, Barzan Ibrahim al-Tikriti, was a whiner and complainer if ever there was one. Formerly in charge of the greatly feared Iraqi secret police, the Mukhabarat, he was brutal and confrontational. You may have correctly deduced he wasn't very popular among the Americans.

I read something on the Internet recently to the effect that he had cancer while he was in captivity, but I knew nothing about it.

Barzan Ibrahim al-Tikriti

BARZAN IBRAHIM HASAN
AL-TIKRITI
Presidential Advisor

As far as I knew, he was relatively healthy. Knowing him as I did, he would have said something. He wasn't one to suffer in silence.

You may recall his particularly grisly execution when his head was actually severed from his body when he was dropped through the trap door. Some people thought at first it was because he was so heavy, but he wasn't heavy at all. Hangings are done with a length of rope calculated using the prisoner's weight, and there is a specific drop, usually between four and ten feet. Too long a drop can lead to decapitation.

Barzan was part of the (formerly) ruling Sunni minority, and the Shia are now getting their revenge. That's why many of us think the beheading was done deliberately, just not with a knife. "I bet they added a foot of rope," Adams said. "He was widely hated."

He certainly didn't make life any easier for Adams, who said that Barzan was always an instigator of issues such as hunger strikes, which they loved to stage. Barzan denied any involvement until Adams put him in an isolation cell and told him he wasn't going to get out until he called off the hunger strike. He lasted an hour or so and then the hunger strike was over.

After one particular strike that we figured was not serious, and after their cells were tossed (searched), the guards found and confiscated a lot of food the detainees had been squirreling away. Nobody refused breakfast the next morning. These guys were a bunch of wimps. When Saddam went on a hunger strike, he went on a hunger strike.

By the way, "tossing their cells" is something we did regularly. Every two weeks "tiger teams" went through the cells looking for anything that the detainees should not have had. The teams were made up of people who did not work in the prison. They were in the same units as the inside guards, but their primary duty was to provide escort service.

Using guards from outside the prison was Adams' idea. He said it was better if the regular guards did not conduct the searches, in case some of the detainees would get their noses out of joint and then maybe seek revenge. The tiger teams came up with some surprising items. One time they found several strands of wire woven together, probably from some construction debris that one of the detainees found in his cell, and collected enough to make what could have been used as a weapon, to stab either a guard or another detainee.

The tiger teams were also looking for pills. The detainees would hoard pills, and we feared they might accumulate enough to commit suicide. In a few cases when certain detainees were on multiple doses of a medication that needed to be given more than once daily, we would give them a packet in the morning with instructions for the rest of the day. They knew the drill, and we simply didn't have time to make several trips to various cells to administer all those medications. We didn't do this for everyone and mostly we knew which ones we could trust. Still, we wanted to make sure no one was saving medicines or giving it to his buddy to use as a possible overdose, thus cheating the hangman.

* * *

SULTAN HASHEM AHMED AL-JABBOURI AL-TAI WAS ONE DETAINEE we weren't fattening up for the kill. We were slimming him down. The Eight of Hearts in the Deck of Cards, Sultan was the former minister of defense and was chief of the Al-Anfal operation in which thousands of Iraqi Kurds were killed during the Iran-Iraq War. Considered one of the most courageous officers during the Iran-Iraq War, Sultan was decorated for this by Saddam Hussein. As evidence of what I consider to be the incestuous regime—which apparently Saddam considered necessary in order to keep loyal and trustworthy people around him—I note that one of Sultan's daughters was married to Qusay Hussein, Saddam's second son.

Sultan negotiated and signed the ceasefire with Norman Schwarzkopf, the commander in chief of the U.S. Central Command

Sultan at his arraignment.

8 ♥

127

SULTAN HASHIM AHMAD AL-TAI
Minister of Defense

♠
8

during the Gulf War. Sultan was turned over to the Iraqi interim government on June 30, 2004, and along with Chemical Ali was the first to be arraigned in the Iraqi court on July 1. In September 2003, Sultan had turned himself in after negotiating a promise to release him after investigations were completed. I think he planned to cooperate with the coalition against Chemical Ali or maybe even Saddam.

In my reading since returning to the States, it appears that the general was widely thought to be willing to help bring the war to a quick end and to ensure a postwar peace. In fact, he was seen on Iraqi television making what some interpreted as a thinly disguised suggestion not to fight the invaders.

It was also rumored that Paul Bremer, the administrator of the Coalition Provisional Authority, asked Sultan to be the new president of Iraq, because Bremer thought he commanded so much respect. Apparently, Sultan turned down the offer; I have no independent knowledge of that. What I can speak to is our success in getting some of his weight off. He weighed 327 pounds when he got to Camp Cropper, and on the Camp Cropper diet he dropped 100 pounds. As I recall, we adjusted his portions. Plus, he got no snacks and couldn't eat between meals.

I was told he wrote home, pleased with his health care and proud that he had lost the weight. True Story told me that Sultan wasn't the only one who wrote home about how pleased he was at having lost weight and how much healthier he felt. Many detainees were forty to fifty pounds overweight when they came to us.

It fell to Sergeant Major Ken Carpenter to deal with the detainees' letters, both outgoing and incoming. They could write one letter a week and only to a close relative. Sometimes, if they were especially cooperative with the interrogators, they might be allowed more. The mail was picked up and delivered by the Red Cross. The reason they were so limited in the number of letters they could send wasn't punitive; it was because reading and translating so many letters was time-consuming. And everything had to be read and translated, for obvious reasons.

Carpenter said he got a completely different perspective on the detainees because of reading those letters. "No matter how ruthless these guys were, they were still somebody's dads or, more likely, granddads whose grandchildren looked up to them. You still knew they were bad people, but you couldn't help feeling sorry for the families. By reading those letters you saw them as human beings," he said.

Ken said the families would write about losing their homes and how they were living with relatives in order to survive. And the detainees had all this information, but there was nothing they could do. Formerly powerful men who were used to snapping their fingers and making things happen were now totally helpless.

I understand what he means. When you are thousands of miles away from people being captured and killed, you are removed from the whole process. But when you are there, up close, seeing the faces of these people, the effects of the war takes on more immediacy and becomes more personal. I admit it sometimes became somewhat personal for me, although I think I developed ways to protect myself from getting overly involved, most of the time.

Sometimes detainees would ask us to intervene, most often to supply them with more information about the fate of their families. We couldn't help them, of course, but sometimes their obvious anxiety got to us. In particular, I remember one stout fellow with a full beard who had the most astonishingly peaceful look on his face. I don't know why that struck me, but it did. Obviously, he wasn't one of the "highest value" detainees—he certainly wasn't in the Deck of Cards—but somebody must have thought he had some information our government wanted. Despite his outward demeanor I knew he was truly hurting inside. Plus, he had frequent crying episodes.

Amazingly, he told me he wasn't angry with the United States for invading; he just wished they hadn't bombed his house and killed his wife and two daughters. I thought that more than anything he needed someone to talk to. I told him that I could see he was in a lot of pain, and I think he appreciated that. I offered to arrange for him to talk to a psychiatrist, and then I worked out the details; about every two weeks I picked up an Army shrink from the 785th Combat Stress Hospital. The psychiatrist, a female major, saw this guy and several others. When she left because of an emergency back home, she was replaced. I can only hope the program continued after we left. As you can imagine, there were lots of emotional issues associated with being detained no matter how well we treated these people.

Another showed me a picture of his wife and two kids—a boy and a girl. It was fairly early one morning, and I was passing out medication. He started to cry as he pulled a picture out of his pocket. His wife was a very attractive woman, and the kids were beautiful. All he wanted was to know if they were okay. Not unreasonable, I thought. I told him I just did medicine, but I would send his request up the chain of command. I tried to follow up on all these requests, but I had so much to do and never learned what happened. I hope the International Committee for the Red Cross (ICRC) was able to help him.

As I made my rounds, I often carried drugs in my pocket, including syringes filled with morphine and Toradol in my breast pocket. If someone was in severe pain, I didn't want to be running back to the clinic. One thing I didn't ever have was a stethoscope around my neck. I would have been setting myself up to be strangled.

On one occasion, a suspected assassin complained loudly of back pain. He was eager when he learned I had morphine available to partake on the spot. Then he asked how big the needle was, and when I showed him his back pain suddenly subsided. I still had the cap on the needle and I grabbed his arm and said, "Come on, man up. Man up." But he said "no" and I never took the cap off the needle. Some of those guys were total wimps.

One guy, brought to us from Abu Ghraib, couldn't stand solitary confinement. He cried, wet his pants, banged his head on the wall, wanted out, wanted to see his family. I kept notes on him to make sure we weren't accused of abuse. I wanted to say, again, "Man up." When they put him in a group room he was much better. Then when they wanted to squeeze more information out of him, they put him back in solitary. Eventually, they sent him back to Abu Ghraib.

I guess Camp Cropper was the country club of the POW camps. People seemed to want to come here. In fact, an Australian jihadist told me that he had been promised the "hotel prison." I guess this was better than any other place he could have gone. This guy made me laugh. He told me he had been out on his wedding night and was picked up for nothing. I said to him, "You were out on your wedding night! Give me a break." I can think of several other things he could have been/should have been doing on his wedding night.

George Piro remembers calling Cropper "the petting zoo," at the same time noting that it was a model facility. On more than one occasion we in the 439th referred to it as a retirement home. By midsummer, Colonel Sylvester and crew re-engineered schedules to allow the detainees to have extra time outside in the evening hours. We called these periods "garden parties," and they were held in the courtyard between buildings. I think they got as much as four hours in the cooler air. That made the ICRC very happy.

The interim Iraqi government officials, however, complained that the conditions were much too good, especially in light of the conditions found in Saddam's prisons. Consistent power, clean water, daily medical care, and exercise were all provided, and the Iraqi officials point out that these accommodations surpassed those found in homes of the average Iraqis, according to Colonel Sylvester.

Obviously, this was a much better place than Abu Ghraib. For one thing we had the benefit of good leadership, and, despite the amount of work we had to do to keep the place running, Colonel Sylvester was aware of all that was going on. He and his designates always were in control.

At Camp Cropper, the prisoners all ate what we ate—except for pork products—and eventually everyone had air-conditioning, although it was an old, finicky system that went out at inopportune times. These occasional breakdowns were not surprising, considering the extreme heat and the fact that in many months it was running 24-7. I'm very aware of the status of the air-conditioning, because the clinic was the last place to get AC, and that was after the trial started in July 2004.

I didn't dwell on it then, and I don't think my colleagues did either, but occasionally we were smacked in the face by the fact that here we were, reservists from the U.S. Heartland, in charge of most of the leadership of the former Iraqi regime, starting with Saddam. We worked hard and I think proved our mettle, but it still blows my mind when I stop and think about the major responsibility—the awesome responsibility, really—that we had. Logically, this work should have fallen to an active duty unit.

"We happy few" were fortunate in more ways than one, and chief among these was the fact that we were reservists and that we all had other life experiences that proved to be valuable. True Story, in charge of security, is a police chief in real life, for instance. Ron Adams had been the assistant regional security officer for the Department of Commerce (central region) before his retirement, a few months before our deployment. And our executive officer—Major K, we called him—was a power-line electrical engineer who built power lines for a living. Colonel Sylvester, who in his other life worked as a defense contractor for Northrop Grumman Corp., gave Major K major credit for solving many of our problems with the heating and air-conditioning systems.

This sort of diversity, according to Sylvester, was probably what made our mission so particularly successful. At least we thought we were successful, and apparently others did too: we got many accolades from higher headquarters including the Pentagon, the ICRC, and the Department of Defense. Their review of our program was summed up with, "Keep doing what you're doing."

5 | MR. CLEAN FEEDS THE BIRDS

"**I**F YOU STAY HERE, I CAN TEACH YOU ARABIC IN SIX MONTHS," Saddam once promised me, and I wish to this day that I could have had that opportunity—to learn Arabic, that is.

It would be a valuable skill these days; good for the old resume, as we used to say. Actually, during my tour I attended a class in Arabic at Camp Cropper that was taught by one of our interpreters. We learned the alphabet, and we were beginning to construct sentences when my duties took me away from the classroom, which was just a tent we had set up outside the compound where the detainees were housed. Our instructor was a Kurd named Salaar.

From another interpreter, I learned some of the bad words that would get you into a fight. I guess he wanted us to know how bad they were so we could be prepared to fight or run if we used them. I wrote those down.

Like Hebrew, Arabic is read from right to left. I had never thought about it, but it became clear to me one day in the clinic when we were giving vision tests to some of the detainees. They read a chart right to left, and we were judging them left to right. We finally caught on.

But since leaving Iraq, I have often wondered if I could have communicated better with Saddam—and all the detainees—if I had spoken Arabic. I sense we might have had some interesting conversations. I think Saddam would have had a lot to say, especially about the political climate. He also knew a lot about the history of his country going back to when it was Mesopotamia, the cradle of civilization. He seemed to take pride in the history.

He also talked about other things that I am sure were important, including Iraq's high water table and how you only need to dig down eighteen inches or so before you hit water. He said the area to the north was prettier and greener. The way he described it made me want to go there.

We weren't supposed to engage in political discussions or information gathering, but even with those constraints I'm sure I could have learned a lot from him. Saddam had missed out on a lot of formal education in his early, impoverished childhood, but somewhere along the way he had managed to get a law degree. In addition, he was clearly smart, especially street smart.

I had long since gotten over my initial concern that I might have to wrestle Vic if he attempted to escape. I didn't think there was any danger and that he was certainly not about to attempt such a thing. Since he was completely isolated, he certainly couldn't think about leading a takeover of Camp Cropper. I'm sure he had sized up the situation and concluded there was no escaping, so he might as well make the best of it.

I was under another misconception, which was that Saddam must have surely figured his incarceration was just a matter of time. After all, he had been jailed before and even sentenced to death at least once, before escaping. We even talked about that. He said, "They want me to be in jail, okay, I'll be in jail. I've been in jail four times and each time, the time it go . . ." and he raised his hand at different levels, each time going higher. From that I interpreted that each incarceration had grown increasingly longer.

However, George Piro said that Saddam did not expect to ever be released, and, furthermore, he had something to prove by standing firm, by not running to a safe haven, and by allowing himself to be executed. "We talked about it many times," George said. "He wanted to secure his place in history, to be viewed as remaining defiant: to be viewed as Saddam the Warrior, Saddam the Hero—that sort of image, versus being meek or a coward."

Meanwhile, he seemed to adjust very well doing rather mundane things and enjoying very simple pleasures. One of my favorite images of Saddam is when the birds came flocking as soon as he appeared in the dusty plot of ground we called the rec area. He would save bread from his meals and would throw the crumbs out. Birds would be sitting on the concertina wire waiting. As soon as he emerged, they came swooping down. They were small birds, probably sparrows. He would say, "Look. They come," making an expansive gesture with his hands. Those birds seemed to make him really happy. I thought of the Bird Man of Alcatraz on those occasions, although I didn't mention that to him. I doubt if he would have appreciated the comparison and likely didn't know anything about Burt Lancaster, who will always be the Bird Man to me.

One day no birds came. He shrugged. "They must have eaten earlier," was all he said, but his voice was tinged with sadness. That only happened once. The next day the birds were back, lining up eagerly, ready to pounce on their daily bread.

He also tried to garden in this same dusty plot. What he was tending appeared to be just a pitiful patch of weeds, but maybe he knew something that I didn't. In fact, I have since learned that George had asked his mother to send some seeds, so maybe it wasn't all in vain. Saddam seemed proud: "This is my garden," he said once, as he was watering the sorry, scrubby stuff next to the building. "When I grew up, I always had a garden. I never forget how I grew up . . . a poor farmer."

He watered regularly with a garden hose that Adams bought for him. Previously Saddam had been using a sprinkling can, but George took it away from him. He was fearful that some part of it could be used as a weapon.

Along with writing and reading, these were more active ways of coping and trying to add some normalcy to his confinement. Feeding birds and making a garden are creative ways of spending time when you're locked up. I often wonder why some people seem to make good adjustments to adverse conditions such as prison. George's theory was that Saddam's adjustment had something to do with his tough childhood.

I tend to think it had more to do with the force of his personality and his own strong ego that allowed him to like himself. I also wonder if in some weird way that prison wasn't almost a relief, if he simply was tired. "He told me that he never stayed in the same place for more than a night," George said. "He was constantly on the move and he was also comfortable being by himself, which is key when you're incarcerated."

Sometimes I had a hard time reconciling the formerly powerful dictator with the cooperative man who was so dependent on us for everything from the time of day to his trips to the latrine. The concept that the care of this man, who once had absolute power over roughly 27 million people and now was entrusted to me, was brought home by a simple incident involving, of all things, wet wipes.

At the time it happened, it struck me as an amusing irony, but then I forgot about it until going over my notes recently. Obviously, I had a variety of stuff going on that day. From my journal of everything I needed to do on a typical day of multitasking:

Get forklift from 118th, blood draw for #s 34, 86, 75, 78; sick call #65, shoulder injection; #42 knee pain; #70 cough with chest pain; #17, chest pain; #73 anxiety; #21 & #83 dental, wet wipes for Vic.

The forklift was for moving pallets of sandbags to reinforce the Hesco Barriers, and I worked on that project after I finished my nursing duties, which took most of the rest of the day. From late afternoon until dark, we unloaded sandbags. The added barriers were to fortify the trailers, which never could have withstood a mortar attack. Then I headed back to the clinic to get the wet wipes for Saddam. He had mentioned the previous evening that he needed some. I found a small box and, after a quick shower, I took him the wet wipes. He looked at the box skeptically and pulled out one wipie, holding it between his index finger and thumb. He looked at it for a bit. "These are kind of" . . . he groped for a word. . . "dainty," he finally said.

Dainty. I swear he used that word. That's what I mean about his English being as good as he wanted it to be. Had he slipped up or was he simply feeling more comfortable around me?

I nodded in understanding, and I winked: "You want something man-sized," I said. We both laughed. I explained that this would have to do for now because they were all we had, but I could try to find some bigger wet wipes and come back later. At that point it was about 8 p.m. He said something to the effect that it could wait until "tomorrow."

The next day I found him some more—two boxes of man-sized wet wipes. He was a notorious clean freak, and he apparently used those wet wipes with abandon. Those and a fly swatter to kill mosquitoes were how he kept things neat and tidy.

"This ought to hold you for a while," I said as he greeted me with his customary handshake.

He smiled at me and chuckled. "Papa Noel," he said. Apparently that's all it took to be his Santa Claus that day.

Poor farmer or not, somewhere along the way he developed a fastidiousness that was not exactly reflected in the picture taken when our forces captured him and pulled him from that hole in the ground, scruffy, unshaven, and undoubtedly dirty. But it certainly is reflected in the pictures taken when he was at the peak of his power and living the sumptuous life he must have led.

Even in prison, he was impeccably clean. He had two *dishdashas*—one white and one gray—and he wore them on alternate days, washing one each day. Adams calls him a "germaphobe," and he's probably right. Saddam could somehow drink water from a bottle, never letting the mouth of the bottle touch his lips. Although I never saw it happen, Adams reported that Saddam always washed his hands after shaking hands with visitors.

Knowing how much Saddam liked to be neat, George arranged for a barber to come in and cut Saddam's hair and trim his beard. Shortly after he was captured, he—or somebody—shaved off his beard. He kept his moustache. The detainees were allowed to shave and even cut their own hair, all under the watchful eyes of the guards, who collected the razors and clippers after the grooming was finished.

Saddam requested, and Adams provided him with, cleaning supplies including a bucket, spray bleach, and Pine-sol, which he used at will to clean his cell. He didn't have a mop, of course. Apparently, Saddam scrubbed his own floor. Once Adams teased me about how I had been captured on a tape "scrubbing Saddam's floor." I wasn't, of course, but was simply wiping up some spilled water. I certainly didn't want to be tracking through that on his clean floor.

There was one unfortunate incident that turned into a bit of an international brouhaha when a picture of Saddam in his underwear, doing his laundry, ended up in *The Sun*, Rupert Murdoch's British tabloid. Someone somehow snuck the picture out of the camp, but it shouldn't have happened. That was an offense for which you can get in a lot of trouble; it's against Geneva Conventions to exploit prisoners of war, and it's against the Uniform Code of Military Justice as well. When I got home, there was an investigation, and everyone from our unit was interviewed by the CID (criminal investigation detachment), which is like the military's FBI. Colonel Sylvester called me to warn about the interview and stressed, "Just tell the truth."

In the meantime, Colonel Sylvester had reviewed the pictures, and it was clear by something in the background that the picture had been taken well before we took over. I told the investigator everything I knew—which wasn't much—and I didn't hear any more about the incident until recently when I heard that indeed someone had been court-martialed. I don't think Saddam ever knew about the incident.

A sorry contrast to Saddam was Tariq Aziz, a man of many titles: former deputy prime minister, foreign minister, and minister of information, the face you often saw on Iraqi television. To us he was No. 25 or the Eight of Spades in the Deck of Cards. In 2004, MSNBC reported that he might have broken and was ready to name names in Iraq's oil-for-food scandal. This same report called him the "sophisticated and intelligent face of a thuggish regime" and noted that he was known for his elegant English suits and fondness for Cuban cigars.

Tariq Aziz

I can attest to the latter, but that's about all. In many ways, he was so different from Saddam that I can hardly imagine them working together. Adams, who had more dealings with him that I did, calls Aziz a pig. I cannot argue.

Every couple of weeks Adams would send in a search team to "toss the cell," which means they were searching for everything from contraband to squirreled-away food. They always found a lot of the latter, and the place stank. He stank, although he was provided with soap and deodorant or anything else in the way of hygiene he might want.

We figured his food stash was probably good insurance against the hunger strikes that the prisoners loved to stage. And when they did, it was usually Tariq Aziz or Barzan—or both—behind them. The hunger strikes usually lasted no more than forty-eight hours or until the food they'd stashed away ran out.

Aziz was a problem from the get-go, according to Adams, who tells a story about how Aziz initially announced that he would speak only to an officer and refused to deal with an enlisted man. Ron told him to put his request in writing, and he took it to the colonel, who laughed and said to tell him, "It's gonna be a long year."

"He (Colonel Sylvester) said that I was his representative and if he didn't deal with me, he wouldn't be dealing with anybody," Ron told me.

Aziz really was a two-bit troublemaker and his antics weren't worthy of a four year old. When bored, he would take off his sandals and throw them at the lights in the ceiling to knock them loose. Just to make trouble. Just to show contempt.

The only non-Muslim in the camp as far as I know, Aziz was a non-practicing Catholic who somehow had wormed his way into the Ba'ath Party. His records showed he had a history of alcohol abuse, but when I asked him if he drank alcohol, he said, "No, it's not permitted." When I mentioned his records, he conceded that, yes, he liked a couple of glasses—preferably Scotch—after dinner.

He also loved junk food. One of the many issues he found to

complain about was the change of eating schedule during Ramadan. During the holiday, Adams, who impressed me with his sensitivity to the religious beliefs of our charges, saw to it that they were fed early—around 5 a.m.—and would then get their dinners after sunset. Then, to make sure they got three meals a day, he would have them given an MRE at midnight. But Aziz didn't like that, and we didn't much care. Adams told him he could save his MRE and eat it any time he wanted. He was being treated just like everybody else. Meanwhile, he sat and puffed on his cigar and watched the rest of the detainees as they prayed.

Tariq was one of several big talkers who liked to rail about the occupation and how bad off the country was. We weren't supposed to be involved in any intelligence gathering, but, first, this wasn't exactly "intelligence," and, second, we weren't questioning, he was just opining. This was his standard speech: "The U.S. has established a puppet government, and it is not accepted by the Iraqi people." He said the suicide bombers, insurgents, and fanatics were all that was left to repel the invaders.

What Aziz didn't talk about was how the United States had dissolved the Iraqi military—a mistake in my view—and now these guys didn't have anything better to do and, of course, no money. They had families too, and no way to support them. So I guess that planting bombs as part of the insurgency was the only game in town. In my opinion, the ripple effect of all those people out of work greatly strengthened the insurgency. And if you don't have any money, and you get paid well for planting an IED, yeah, you're gonna do it.

Aziz's complaints were an annoyance to all of us, especially, I suspect, to the colonel and to Adams, who had to deal with him daily.

On the other hand, Saddam, except for his initial hunger strike, was low maintenance and sometimes an interesting diversion. An evening in early March, when I had to do an EKG on my famous charge, was one such diversion.

The procedure was routine; we even had a personal EKG machine for Saddam, which I kept under my bed in my room. It was portable, but a more modern machine than the one that was kept in the room next to his. It had been a long day and I was tired, but at 8 p.m. I took the machine and headed down to the wood, in truth feeling a little sorry for myself. On this night my colleagues were winding down, chillin' out, but I had this last chore to do. "Oh well," I told myself, "Let's get it over with."

It was a calm, unusually clear, and relatively cool night. My path along the walk was lighted only by a crescent moon. Many, many stars twinkled overhead. I had the EKG machine over one shoulder and was munching from a bag of chips. I ran into Jayhawker (the colonel) on the way, who asked about Victor. "He's fine," I said. "I just have to do an EKG to make sure his heart is okay."

I continued through the sallyport and on to the wood, knocking

Sallyport, the entrance to the compound where the detainees were held. The white building just on the other side of the Hesco Barriers is the clinic, where I spent much of my time.

on the door and announcing myself to the guards at the end of the hall. We walked down the hall together to Victor's room. They unlocked the door to his room, and I saw that he was reading.

He put down his book and greeted me with his customary smile and enthusiastic handshake: straight arm coming at me diagonally to clasp my one free hand. My chips were gone now, but I feared my fingers would be greasy. If they were, he didn't seem to notice and slapped the arm of one of the two plastic chairs in the room to indicate where I should sit. All with great gusto. He was playing host and I was the honored guest. He didn't seem surprised by the EKG machine. I'm sure that George had told Saddam that morning that we were planning the procedure for that evening.

"Good evening," I said as I arrived.

"Hello, Dr. Ellis," he said, sort of winking. I was never sure if he thought he was flattering me by addressing me as a doctor or if he was simply teasing. Whatever, he almost always addressed me as "Dr. Ellis." Later on, I learned for sure he knew my true occupation: his "Nurse Named Alice," as you will recall.

I said he needed to remove his shirt and lie down, but instead he sat down on his cot, unbuttoned a few buttons of his white *dishdasha*, and took his arms out, letting it fall down around his waist. He laid down that way, exposing a very hairy chest. I got out a disposable razor as I tried to explain what I was doing, although he didn't blink at the sight of the razor. "These pads won't stick, so I'm going to shave certain spots," I said. Before I started, however, he put his hand over mine to stop me, and then proceeded to pull the hair from his chest with his fingers. He'd look at me and grin, showing how brave he was.

"Doesn't that hurt?" I asked with an exaggerated grimace. He only laughed a sort of sinister laugh and continued to pull out his own chest hairs. He didn't so much as flinch in the next few minutes he spent at this strange activity, laughing all the while. Eventually he succumbed to the razor, but not before proving how macho he was.

At least, I assume that was the point, but I certainly laughed too.

After the EKG, which was perfectly normal, I gave him his evening meds and checked his blood pressure. It was 164 over 74. I tried not to frown. This was too high, especially considering the relaxed state he was in. We definitely needed to adjust his blood pressure medication, and I made a mental note to discuss this with the doctor.

Then, just for fun, I put the stethoscope in his ears so he could hear the blood rushing through his arteries. He grinned again. "Now I'm the doctor, heh, heh, heh," he said, with the same evil laugh, enjoying our little game.

It was a fun little game we had going, and I was getting into the spirit and relaxing too, but suddenly I was pulled up short by some internal tether. Something was going on inside me, something that demanded identification. It was related to this game of make-believe and the way we were interacting—and, admit it, Ellis, having fun. I was enjoying my time with a mass murderer; I was laughing with a demon. Almost as soon as I identified the feeling, I tried to shake it off and get back into my soldier mode. I gathered my equipment to leave.

"Everything okay?" I asked. He responded in the affirmative, we said our good-byes, and I left, still troubled because it had all been so pleasant.

I began asking myself again: What in the hell are we doing? What does it matter, in the end, what his EKG shows? What does it matter what his blood pressure is? Why are we working so hard to keep this man healthy?

Why am I so bothered tonight? Because, I told myself, I'm a nurse and a soldier. There should be no conflict, but there was. Maybe I enjoyed this evening because Saddam represented the last of my chores before I could go to my own room and relax for the first time since early morning. In fact, I always rather looked forward to seeing him for that very reason. But I couldn't fool myself that easily, and I knew it wasn't the only explanation. The other possibility was maybe that we simply enjoyed each other's company.

I think what I was feeling was guilt for having a good time with this man. If I didn't know his sordid history, I would probably enjoy his company and that would be it. And I could be a good nurse and a good soldier.

It was now past 9 p.m. I had been on the go since about 4:30 a.m., and it was time for some rest and relaxation. I went back to my room, showered, and popped a bag of popcorn in a microwave in a nearby building where most of the unit lived. Then I put in a DVD. I think I watched *Booty Call*—a funny, sexy comedy that took me far, far away from Saddam Hussein.

6 | A BLACKHAWK FOR A STOMACHACHE

ONE NIGHT ABOUT 10:30 P.M., A GUARD CAME TO MY ROOM WITH word that Saddam was asking for me. I was curious, because I had moved from my original quarters, and the doc's room was closer to the wood. In fact, I questioned him to make sure that I was the one Saddam was asking for. But he was clear. "He said 'Ellis,'" the guard said.

Turns out Vic was having abdominal pain. I suggested a couple of remedies, one of which was TUMS. He took the pills I gave him and turned them over in his hand thoughtfully. He said he had given them to his daughter when she had a stomachache. "I break them in half for her," he assured me. At first, I was surprised that something so mundanely all-American was available in Iraq. I concluded that at one time we were so buddy-buddy with his country that we probably gave Saddam anything he needed, including TUMS.

Anyway, I think our relationship took a turn that night. He was calling me instead of the doctor. I think he thought I could make things happen for him, and he saw me as his advocate, someone who could get him things he needed or fix problems for him. Also, I was a consistent presence, as far as medical personnel went; the doctors all rotated out after ninety days and it seemed he felt comfortable with me.

For instance, he had once complained that the guards were making too much noise outside his cell, interfering with his sleep. I think they were making a ruckus playing cards and video games on the computer. I told him I would see what I could do, and when I saw George Piro the next morning, I mentioned the problem. I'm sure George is the one who actually got the guards quieted down. Someone did.

And then there was the honey issue. All the detainees, Saddam included, ate the same food that we ate, which occasionally included pancakes with maple syrup from a little packet. One day, he asked for honey instead. "Honey better than syrup," he said.

I was able to get a couple of jars from the dining facility. We called it the "dfac." They didn't keep it on hand regularly, but they happened to have some the day I checked, so I confiscated it. Then I rationed it, putting it into smaller containers. I'll never forget the look on his face the first time I brought some to him in a small specimen cup that I had sealed. He wore a broad grin as he poured the honey on his pancakes, and he practically smacked his lips as he did so. As he put the first bite in his mouth, it seemed nothing could have made him happier. "Honey much better than syrup," he repeated. He didn't ask for much, so I was glad to help. By then I was sure he trusted me.

I wish the TUMS had been as successful for his stomach pain as the honey was for his mental outlook. Unfortunately, they didn't work. Neither did Maalox or the purple Nexium pills we tried for excess acid production.

Except for that first time, Saddam didn't initiate any more complaints, but when we asked, he let us know that the pain continued. He held both hands on the right side of his upper abdomen and grimaced. That was pretty much the extent of his complaints.

The pain didn't go away, although he was having no nausea or vomiting or diarrhea, and no fever or chills. The pain seemed to be most prevalent after his meals.

By now, a new doctor had rotated in, and one day during his examination he pressed real hard in Saddam's lower abdomen. We call it the inguinal area. It was clearly painful; Saddam sat straight up when it happened, and we had the diagnosis. He had a hernia.

We decided he needed a CT scan, which would necessitate a trip to the CSH. We needed to rule out gallstones, gastric ulcer, appendicitis, among other things. By now, Saddam had been experiencing this low-level pain for about a month; we needed the entire month to get all the necessary clearance, because this was a big, damned deal in terms of coordination, planning, getting necessary approval for equipment, manpower, and air and land transportation, plus contingency plans.

Fortunately, we had Operation Hotel Victor in place, which was essentially a game plan in case Saddam was in dire distress, either very ill or in cardiac arrest for instance, and we needed to transport him. We rehearsed Hotel Victor monthly. These rehearsals ensured that we would not be stumbling and fumbling. We used a stretcher and took all his meds and personal defibrillator in a private ambulance, which was set aside only for Saddam. We did daily maintenance on the vehicle to ensure that the military radio was working, that none of the tires were flat, lights were working, battery charged, oxygen tanks full, and air-conditioning operational. We would contact the Tactical Operations Center, or TOC, saying, "We have a Hotel Victor," and they would, in turn, contact the APOD: "Dogpound, Dogpound (the code name for APOD), we have a Hotel Victor."

Everyone involved would know what that meant. And everyone involved knew his role. While the notification took place, we put a soldier who was standing in for Saddam on the stretcher and into the ambulance, headed out with our two MP escort gun trucks, one in front and one in back and both with mounted .50-caliber machine guns. We drove to the airport to the waiting helicopter. If it had been the real deal, we then would have loaded him into a helicopter and taken him to the CSH. As it turned out, the plan we were contemplating was the real deal, except that it wasn't a true emergency.

Knowing how much effort went into this, I think Operation Hotel Victor was a very good idea. Without it, the trip to the CSH would have been an even bigger deal. The trip, which occurred on the evening of May 16, went off without a hitch. Several of us in the 439th were involved, including Sergeant Major Carpenter, who had to make a preliminary military risk-assessment at the CSH before we took Saddam there.

A trip to the CSH is no joyride, and transporting Saddam was no exception. We were such easy targets that it boggles my mind. For the trip, Saddam was handcuffed, shackled, and blindfolded. He was wearing body armor as well as a helmet. So was I, the doc, and George, who had earlier explained to Saddam what was going on. We proceeded through the exercise yard to a waiting ambulance.

Saddam actually seemed a little nervous and asked if he could bring his Quran. We agreed, but since he couldn't hold it as he climbed into the helicopter, he handed it off to me. That happened again when he was getting out. I bet I was the first infidel to ever hold it.

I knew better than to touch it without being asked, because in our sensitivity training at Fort Riley we were told never to touch a Muslim's Quran. There were several other do's and don't's that we tried to remember as we were dealing with the detainees. For instance, we were told not to cross our legs and show the bottoms of our shoes. It's an insult in Arab culture, since your shoes are considered low and dirty. Throwing shoes is fraught with symbolism: Remember when Saddam's statue came down, and it was pelted with shoes in 2003? Remember when President George W. Bush ducked shoes at his final news conference in Iraq?

Saddam's Quran was important to him. When he wasn't reading it, he placed it on a wooden folding table in his cell along with several other books. But now I was holding the precious book.

Our mission was under way. We were accompanied in the vehicle by two rovers—guards who were roaming the perimeter—in full battle rattle including night-vision goggles. At the APOD, we were met by two Blackhawk helicopters. They were painted black so they would blend with the night sky. We flew in tandem; in case one went down, the other could come to the rescue—at least that's the theory. Also traveling with us was a land escort, a convoy of four gun trucks. I might add here that Saddam was the only detainee for whom they flew the choppers; for others we traveled by land.

Flying at treetop level, I was having visions of *Blackhawk Down*. I could count the lighted windows in the buildings below. "For God's sake, get this thing up a little higher," I wanted to scream. Anybody on a rooftop with a rocket-propelled grenade could take us out. I quickly dismissed the thought, but my palms continued to sweat and I could feel my heart thumping through my body armor.

At 9 p.m., we landed at the CHS. Security was tighter than a brick in a wall. Saddam was placed in a wheelchair and was whisked away into a pre-selected area in the hospital that was supposed to be easily defended in case things went wrong. When he got to the first secured room, he was uncuffed, and the body armor and blindfold were removed.

It was time for the CT scan, which was when things got stupid. The IV that I had started earlier and that had been running fine all day now had to have a companion in the other arm. Why he needed two IV's is beyond me, but everyone seemed to want to touch the famous man, to get in on the action. This included a nurse anesthetist whom Saddam was ogling; she's the one who started the second IV. She did, indeed, have a nice behind, and believe me, Saddam noticed. In fact, his eyes followed her the entire time she was in the room. We were now in the OR, and Saddam was sitting on an operating room table. He couldn't stop staring at this nurse. "You know, it's been about five months since I've had me a woman," he said to me.

The exterior of the CSH

"Yeah, me too," I said, and the sympathy was no pretense on this score.

"You too?" he said, then laughed his rather sinister laugh.

The CT scan was performed with negative findings for gallstones or colicystitis, and surgery was scheduled for a later date. I jumped for joy. Now we could head home.

It was about 10 p.m., and with any luck, we could be back at Camp Cropper by midnight at the latest. But no. There were eight or nine doctors—all Americans—in the room, and three of them decided they needed a full body CT scan to make sure they haven't missed anything.

Before the full body scan, however, the doctors had something else in mind. On the pretext that they were checking his prostate, one after another of those doctors stuck his finger up Saddam's rectum. I can say with certainty that they did three rectal exams in less than five minutes, and I was starting to feel for my patient. I was furious, as a matter of fact. They were probably anticipating their cocktail conversation back in the States: "And then there was the time I actually got to stick it up Saddam Hussein's tight ass. Literally."

Just as I decided I could stand it no longer and was framing my objections, a major who was in charge saw what was happening and called a halt to it. I have a lot of respect for him and also for another doctor with an Italian name who refused to take part in the madness. Saddam just rolled his eyes and said to me, "Can we go now?" We couldn't. There were many more tests and uncomfortable procedures before he was released.

Finally, at 2:10 a.m. we left the CSH and headed for the landing pad, then we boarded the choppers and headed "home" to Camp Cropper. At 4:00 a.m. we were safely back in quarters. The colonels congratulated us on a job well done. It had been a good mission, and, to top it off, it was carried out mostly by the Reservists of the 439th and National Guardsmen from Delta Company, who provided the escorts. Sometimes we were made to feel like second-class citizens,

I take time out at the CSH to pose with Sergeant Pat Crader (left) and Lieutenant Robert Coleman (right), both from my home unit.

so this was a small vindication. Before I fell into bed we had to brief the higher-ups. We did After Action Reports, or AARs, on every mission, and this one had been major. A couple hours later, I was making rounds. When I saw, Vic he was still asleep. I left him alone and didn't see him until my next scheduled visit at 8 p.m.

It was a nice night with a warm, gentle breeze, and I was tired. In fact, I couldn't wait to get to my room and hit the hay. I entered the wood and passed the guard with my customary "hello." Saddam was in his room reading, and, as usual, he offered me a chair.

"I don't like that other place," he said. "It was a bad night." I nodded in agreement. Then he asked if I'd had enough sleep. I said no but added something to the effect that this is all part of my job. I gave him his evening meds, and he thanked me.

"Now you get some sleep," he said.

I smiled to myself as I headed back to my room. My patient is now worried about my well-being. I'm thinking, nobody has worried about *me* in a very long time. I have to admit it felt good.

The hernia repair took place about a month later. Again, I made all the arrangements, but this time I got kicked to the curb because people higher up the chain in headquarters decided they wanted in on the action. Colonel Sylvester laughed about that later. "The first time it was 'Oh, good luck. Let us know.'"

The surgery took place at the CSH, and it was routine. Saddam's recovery was also routine, and he was returned to my care the same day as the surgery. He was a good, compliant patient and complained not at all. I wish all my patients could have been like that. The surgery was successful, and Victor's abdominal pain did not recur.

7 | A Poem
for Rita

ONE DAY, SADDAM ASKED US ABOUT OUR FAMILIES. IT WAS IN THE morning, and Cropper Doc, George Piro, and I were all visiting. Our visits sometimes got a bit social, and this time the conversation turned to me. I told Saddam I had two sons and had recently been married for the second time.

He perked up. "You have two wives?"

I laughed. "Yes, but not at the same time. That's against the law in America."

He chuckled, and because he seemed so interested I promised I'd bring back my wedding pictures when I returned that evening. I did, and we sat side by side on his cot as he looked at the pictures carefully. One showed Rita; my son Robert; me; my sister Beverly; and her husband, Lionel, who also grew up in Pruitt-Igoe. Saddam pointed to each and I told them who they were. He seemed especially fascinated with Lionel, who is a cool dude.

"Him?" he asked. I told him it was my brother-in-law and that he's an entertainer who sings and dances. Lionel is based in Las Vegas with the Original Cornell Günter's Coasters and dresses fit to kill. In the picture, he is wearing a stylish four-button, cream-colored coat with narrow lapels, black pants and shirt, and a yellow and white tie. His shoes, which always match the rest of his attire, are black with yellow stripes. A yellow and black silk handkerchief peaks from his pocket. He keeps his head clean-shaven, and he is wearing sunglasses. Saddam seemed to like Lionel's looks. He pointed to him again, then sat back and smiled.

He picked up the pictures again, and this time he pointed to Rita. "I will write a nice story for her," he said.

The next day he had done exactly that. Actually, it was a short poem about a woman's beauty, comparing her to the stars in the heavens.

Our Wedding. My brother-in-law Lionel Pope is on the left, my sister Beverly Pope is on the far right.

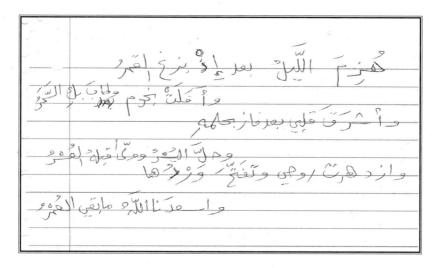

Roughly translated, here's what he wrote:

The night is defeated at the end of life
The stars are getting lost and the dawn is of joy with you
My heart has risen after winning his dream
Comfort is settling and hardship has gone away
My soul had flourished and his flower has matured
And God has blessed us with the remaining of our age.

According to George, most of Saddam's poetry was pretty bad; I guess I had just assumed that the poem suffered in translation. Also, it doesn't make complete sense to me. For instance, after learning from an interpreter that there aren't always comparable words for a translation from Arabic to English, I have another interpretation for the last line: "And God has blessed us for the remaining of our lives." At least that makes sense to me.

He also wrote a poem for the Cropper Doc, who had two young boys at home. This one was about a father's love for his sons.

Sometimes during our meetings we talked about the differences in Iraqi and American culture. We also talked about death. I couldn't help but feel that the Iraqis are much more prone to embrace death than we are. I don't think that's necessarily a good thing, maybe because of the apparent ease with which suicide bombers are recruited.

During one of those discussions, I found an opening to say something about Saddam's two sons, Uday and Qusay, who had died in a shoot-out with Coalition forces the year before. One report I read said that Qusay's fourteen-year-old son also died in the same incident.

I'd wanted an opportunity to say something appropriate about—to acknowledge, really—his sons' deaths, and I figured this was my opening. "I, too, have two sons," I said. "And I grieve for you."

He surprised me: "No cry for my sons; I'm happy for them," he said. I suspect he was proud that they died fighting the invaders and that they died as martyrs. He went on to kiss his hand and make a sort of waving gesture. "I kiss the wind," he said.

I haven't a clue what he meant. Maybe he meant that you can't hold the wind and that you can't just reach out and retrieve whatever it's bearing. And so he couldn't reach out and bring back his sons. Maybe the wind will bear his wishes to them in the afterlife. Maybe it's an Arabic expression that I simply don't know.

Actually, I knew that his sons were loose canons, and I think he did too. Maybe he didn't want to bring them back. "Ruthless, crazy, and arrogant," my friend Ken Carpenter called them. "If his sons had gained power, the Middle East would really have been in trouble," he said recently. "They would have attacked everybody and anybody."

Actually, I think Victor knew that too. In fact, he'd been so angry with Uday back in the late 1980s that he had him jailed for forty days. The reason for his anger was that Uday had got drunk and bludgeoned to death Saddam's favorite food taster, bodyguard Kamel Hana Jajjo.

On the subject of Saddam's sons, George deliberately pressed him during his interrogations, in an attempt to break down his defenses. George says that as Saddam was pressed, he finally had enough and said, in effect, to leave him alone about his sons: "You don't get to pick your kids. You're stuck with what you're given. And this is what I had."

Nice guy, that Uday. I've read how once Uday lost it at a party and killed Saddam's bodyguard in front of whatever unfortunate guests happened to be around. The party, by the way, was honoring Suzanne Mubarak, wife of Eqyptian President Hosni Mubarak. Seems that Uday was angry at Jajjo because he had introduced Saddam to the woman who would become his second wife—a younger wife that Uday considered an insult to his mother. I also read that Uday's mother may have put him up to this.

The second wife, Samira Shahbandar, married Saddam in 1986, after Vic forced her husband to divorce her. He didn't tell me that; I read it. There is a persistent rumor—sometimes stated as fact—that the two had one son, Ali Hussein, who was born in 1983. Maybe to protect him, the family has denied that Ali is Saddam's son but is, in fact, his grandson. I've also read that Saddam's eldest daughter, Raghad Hussein, has claimed that Ali is her son. I have read rumors that he is in a Swiss boarding school, and then I have also read that he is hiding in Syria or Lebanon. At any rate, the kid is probably at high risk, and it's probably just as well that his existence is kept a bit murky and out of the public domain. Maybe one day he will find the world situation changed and he can write his own book.

I have also read rumors that Saddam had two other wives, but I can't substantiate that.

Uday and Qusay were both products of Saddam's first marriage to Sajida Khairallah Tulfah, his first cousin. He met her for the first time when they wed in Eqypt in 1958. Saddam and Sajida had five children—the two infamous sons and three daughters. His other daughters are Rana and Hala.

Uday eventually wormed his way back into his father's radar, if not affections, but Qusay, the younger of the two sons, had by then become the Heir Apparent. Uday had to settle for being the head of Iraq's Olympic Committee and later the head of one of Saddam's security organizations. In the former role, Uday was said to order and oversee the torture of athletes who, according to him, did not perform well. He supposedly kept a scorecard with written instructions on how many times the athlete should be beaten after the athletic event.

The punishments were unbelievable. Among other allegations, athletes were caned on the soles of their feet, which was both painful and didn't leave visible marks. One defector claimed that after failing to reach the 1994 World Cup finals, soccer players were forced to kick a concrete ball. Another said athletes were dragged through a gravel pit and then immersed in a sewage tank so that the wounds would become infected.

I don't blame the father for not trusting this son.

Uday was also known for his raging sexual appetite. One of the younger detainees told us about accompanying Uday to sporting events and how they would scan the crowd with binoculars looking for pretty girls. When they spotted one that Uday liked, the detainee would get her and bring her back to Uday. This detainee was a worker bee rather than a decision-maker. Still, he must have had information our military wanted. His presence at Cropper would indicate that. If he knew what happened to any of these young girls, we weren't privy to it. But from what I have read, it wasn't pretty. These young women probably were ruined for life if they—or their families—were lucky enough to live.

I have no way of knowing how Saddam really felt about his sons, but I get the feeling he truly loved his daughters. Recently, I saw a picture of Raghad, who was a beautiful woman. She was wearing a white shawl over her head, but it only partially covered her light brown hair, and her face was entirely exposed. The picture appeared with an article in USA Today, dated August 2003, after she, her sister Rana Hussein, and their mother had received sanctuary in Jordan.

Despite the fact that Saddam is credited with ordering their husbands killed in 1996, they tearfully described him as a good, loving father with a "big heart." I have also read that Chemical Ali was responsible for killing Saddam's sons-in-law, who were also Chemical Ali's nephews. I also read they were killed by "fellow clan members." I suspect that Saddam's daughters, at least, preferred to blame anyone but their father. And I also suspect that Saddam and his advisors had reason not to trust the sons-in-law. Hussein Kamel, who was married to Raghad, and his brother, Saddam Kamel, Rana's husband, were considered traitors. Apparently, they were sharing weapons secrets with such agencies as UNSCOM, the CIA, and MI6 and also planning an insurrection against Saddam's regime.

While Saddam was on the lam after the U.S. invasion, his daughters did not know his whereabouts. At the same time, an audiotape attributed to Saddam was circulating in which he was urging Iraqis to join the anti-American insurgency even as he was vowing to return to power "at any moment," according to a story in USA Today.

About that time, Raghad told CNN that the message she wanted to send her father, "I love you and I miss you." Rana was quoted as saying that Saddam was "very tender" with all his children and that she felt closer to him than to her mother. The daughters, who had nine children between them, also said that those closest to Saddam had betrayed him.

After that first conversation about families, Saddam never discussed his sons again, but, ironically, even as everyone was gearing up for his trial and he knew he was facing possible execution, he talked several times about wanting to father more children. I think he probably did like children. Maybe he simply liked the idea of strengthening his lineage, of having more children to carry on his name.

He discussed this with me and also with Cropper Doc. We told him the facts of life and how a woman loses her eggs as she ages. We also tried to explain that, given his present situation, it was next to impossible. I think we got our point across, and we tried to do it delicately. We did all this with the help of George, serving in the capacity as Saddam's interpreter.

Vic was stoic and seemed to be processing the information, nodding in understanding as the explanations went on. If he felt anger, he didn't show it. He only showed a slight disappointment. Forget a younger woman; he must have known he wasn't going to get a woman, period, at Camp Cropper.

8 | A BEHEADING ON TELEVISION

ONE DAY WE TOOK A BREAK, WHICH WE NEEDED DESPERATELY. Since we were ourselves in sort of lockdown mode, we always grabbed the chance to get outside Camp Cropper, and once we got outside we tried to make the best use of our time.

On these occasions, we usually had a grocery list from others back at camp. I was looking in a little store we called "the hadji shop" for some DVDs for one of the interpreters. I also planned to pick up a couple for myself. You could get them cheap. Sometimes there are four movies on one DVD, and you could get two for five dollars or maybe less.

I was alone in the shop when I happened to look up at a television that was mounted in a corner near the ceiling. Two employees were watching too. I saw a guy holding a big knife, and he was pulling a man outside a red and white striped tent. The victim's hands were tied behind his back and he had started trying to run away, saying "la, la, la, la, la," which means "no" in Arabic. But someone tackled him and held his feet and another straddled his body, grabbing a handful of his hair. He stopped screaming, and a look came over his face that I can only describe as resignation. He closed his eyes and within ten seconds they were holding his head in the air as pools of blood spilled out into the street. People on the sidewalk stepped over the blood and kept going as if nothing had happened.

I was dumbstruck. I simply could not believe I was standing there watching this. On television. Nobody seemed to be at all affected at seeing a man lose his head right there on the sidewalk.

Right after this, the owner of the shop walked in and screamed at the employees for having the television on. Obviously, he didn't think watching this public beheading was good for business, since most of his business came from American soldiers. I never knew if anyone else saw it or not.

I also wondered how the television station got it so quickly. There was someone with a camcorder right there, filming the whole thing. I even saw someone filming the guy who was doing the filming.

Needless to say, this was a big topic of conversation back in the camp that night. Suddenly, we felt we had come face to face with what we were dealing with here in Iraq. We all knew we were treading in dangerous waters, but this brought it home in a new and immediate way. Beheading seems to be the favored method of execution if someone takes a dislike to you around here.

It wasn't the first time we had been exposed to this gruesome way of meting out punishment. As part of our training, we had seen videos of people getting part of their tongues cut off, their arms broken, and worse. One of the videos showed a young kid with all the hair shaved from his head; he'd been blindfolded and set on a donkey backwards with sign around his neck in Arabic, which we couldn't read. He was paraded around town, and crowds turned out to watch. Then he was caned and beaten to a pulp with maybe one hundred lashes.

In another segment, they took people to the top of a high building and threw them off; some jumped before the captors had the chance to throw them. I remember one victim was wearing a Superman T-shirt. Don't ask me to explain that one, and I can assure you he wasn't leaping tall buildings in a single bound. At the bottom, an ambulance picked them up. I guess if they were unlucky enough to survive they went to some sort of prison; otherwise, they went to a morgue.

The ultimate punishment, I presume, is to lose one's head. We were shown that too. They had this poor bloke on a loading dock. They made him lie down and positioned him so that his head was even with the edge of the platform. A guy straddled him, sat on his back, and pulled the victim's legs up, holding them under his arms. A second man came with a sword. The first blow seemed to be a good hit, but it didn't sever the head. He seemed to miss the neck on the follow-up, hitting the back of the victim's shoulders instead. Finally, a third person approached with a knife. I think he was tired of the swordsman's incompetence. The knife-wielder was more efficient, he sawed a couple of times, then set the severed head on the man's shoulders.

This video was shown to us shortly after we got to Iraq. It was unnerving, but I said to myself, "Well, that's how they do business over here."

Much more unnerving was the one I saw on television, and it was more efficient than in the film. There was nothing sloppy about it. It took maybe ten seconds, but it had a far greater impact on me. It just blew my mind that the victim seemed so resigned, so accepting of his fate. And this was real life, not a training film.

To say our anxiety was ratcheted up a few notches after my experience in the hadji shop is a bit of an understatement. We talked more about what had happened to the American Nick Berg, who wasn't even a military guy and was the first person we knew about to die so horribly and publicly a couple of months earlier.

We talked about how we most decidedly didn't want this to happen to us, and we all came to the same conclusion that nobody was going to kidnap us and take us anywhere and cut off our heads. We would stand and fight and die right on the spot if necessary.

In fact, I made a promise not only to myself but also to an

Iraqi-American interpreter that I'll call Matt who accompanied me and No. 79 to the CSH a few days after the beheading incident on television. No. 79 was a detainee who had been complaining about his bad vision, and at the CSH he had been diagnosed with macular degeneration. He was hardly grateful and demanded that we do more, which seriously pissed us off because that particular day we were really risking our necks. There had been more car bombs and sniper fire than usual on Route Irish, which was both the most dangerous and the quickest way to the Green Zone. I'm sure we showed our irritation. "We brought you here. You've been checked out. We can't do any more," Matt said. As it turned out, we would have enough trouble just getting back to Camp Cropper.

We were getting a bit cynical because, as I mentioned earlier, we often suspected some detainees made up complaints just to get out of camp. Even going to the hospital was a field trip for them—a

Route Irish, the world's most dangerous road, is only twelve kilometers long. The black spots are from the dirty window. We never dared to lower the windows when traveling this road.

field trip for which we were risking our necks. Sometimes I wanted
to tell them, "Just suck it up." What a bunch of hypochondriacs.
I understood these guys were bored and had no contact with the
outside world. They were probably not thinking they'd get killed
along with us.

These men had been important people in their previous lives,
catered to and pampered, and, despite their present restrictions,
some clearly weren't past that. As I said, we took complaints of chest
pains seriously, but more than half the time when we took their
vital signs everything was normal. They had headaches and other
complaints. During Ramadan, the fasting seemed to explain many of
the symptoms. But when we offered medicine, they'd refuse, saying it
was Ramadan and they were fasting. No wonder we sometimes felt
we were going in circles.

It was early afternoon when we finished at the CSH with No. 79,

Driving our Humvee through one of Baghdad's many neighborhoods.

and a quick status check made it clear there was too much activity—more car bombs and snipers—on Route Irish for our return trip to the camp. Route Tampa was determined to be the best route back, and we reluctantly set out on it knowing it would take more than twice as long and would take us through bad neighborhoods, including Sadr City.

I'd had at least one bad experience in Sadr City, and I wasn't looking to repeat it. On that occasion, traffic was gridlocked, and this is a place where you don't want to be stationary for too long. In fact, we were under orders not to stop for anything until we got to where we were going. A traffic snarl is more than irritating; it is dangerous. I was trying to watch every building, window, doorway, and rooftop, searching for anyone with an RPG or other weapon. As usual, we were in a convoy of four gun trucks.

It was sheer suicide to remain sitting there. We knew we had to get out of there, so we blew our horns and started nudging the cars out of our way. The few we actually hit could submit claims to the Army. There was a program set up for this very purpose. It seemed totally reckless, but there was nothing else to do.

I felt like I was in a movie. We were driving on sidewalks, into oncoming traffic, on the medians, and plowing down shrubs. "Can't afford to be sitting ducks," we said to ourselves. Someone clever could have set it to music. We were locked and loaded, but one RPG could have ruined the day.

Now I was in Sadr City for the second time. It's a Shiite slum of about 2 million people, where the fearsome al-Sadr Brigade is based. These are militiamen loyal to the radical Shiite cleric Muqtada al-Sadr, and after Saddam's fall, the al-Sadr Brigade gained power and took on a policing role. They were a big part of the insurgency. They hated Saddam, and although they were once friendly to the Americans, by now they hated both us and the Sunnis.

God forbid, we ran into some of them. They are identified by their black clothing and green markings on their masks and headbands.

The first one I noticed was a man in black and green walking on the side of the road near our Humvee. Then our turret gunner spotted another and shouted, "Hey, this guy has an AK," referring to someone in a white Mercedes that had pulled alongside us. The driver indeed had an AK-47 that he just raised up and showed to us in a sign of power, I guess. Now they were on both sides of us. Some in pickup trucks, some in cars, some on foot, swarming like insects. I don't know to this day where they came from or why, but all of a sudden, they were everywhere. We were surrounded.

Under the rules of engagement, we couldn't do a thing. At least we didn't think we could. As Colonel Sylvester pointed out, the rules of engagement changed so frequently that there were times they changed from when we started down Route Irish until we returned. Our rules of engagement regarding the al-Sadr Brigade changed often as well. For instance, when we first arrived in Iraq, they were the enemy and we were supposed to shoot. Later, it was "don't shoot 'em at all." At this point, the rules we were going by stated, "Don't shoot unless they shoot first," and I was ready to shoot. My finger was on the trigger, but my palms were sweating. I was surprised I could hear anything besides the thumping of my heart.

Heart is something that Matt had a lot of. He never refused a mission, and neither did I. But he was scared now. "Don't let 'em get me, Master Sergeant," he said. "Don't let them cut my neck."

"Matt, if it comes to that, I'll do us both," I told him. And I would have. But I soon realized that if they actually attacked us, I wouldn't be able to deter them. All I had was a 9 mm handgun and four magazines, and if we would have engaged in a fight I wouldn't have lasted very long. I vowed I'd never again go to the CSH without my M-16, for which I could carry two hundred rounds of ammunition.

Once more, we lucked out. They didn't shoot at us, and we didn't shoot at them. I'll take that anytime. I think they were just messing with us. They also must have known that if they did engage, we had

Leaving the CSH

a lot of firepower to return. We had four gun trucks with .50-caliber machine guns mounted on top. Those machine guns could take down a house if you have enough ammunition.

As suddenly as they came, they left, and our coast appeared to be clear. We heaved several sighs of relief as we tried to get our breathing back to normal and stilled our excessively beating hearts. We prayed for no more excitement for the rest of the trip. But the experience was a setback for me and, I suspect, the others. Ever since Abu Ghraib, the notorious prison where Americans were shown to be abusing prisoners, we could not afford the slightest bit of bad publicity and we had to react to every hangnail and pimple. Does No. 79's macular degeneration deserve all this fuss? Do the aches and pains of the prisoners who are probably going to be executed need to take precedence over everything? Do they deserve our putting our own lives on the line for them?

9 | THE FIVE OF HEARTS

Huda Ammash, known in the popular press as Mrs. Anthrax and at Camp Cropper as Chemical Sally, came to the clinic for her monthly checkup. She was one detainee I actually liked. She was polite, didn't whine or complain, and had been known to brag that "Iraqi women are tough." Her implication, if I understood her correctly, was that the men were not tough.

An academic and scientist, she had documented and reported on the rise of cancers and birth defects in Iraq after the first Gulf War. Huda also was a fitness freak and made a point of keeping herself in top form and her weight low.

One of the things I liked about her was that, unlike most of her colleagues, she had a sense of humor. On this particular day, I stood behind her and put my foot on the scale as she was getting weighed. She was not happy with the results. "This could not be right; I know I don't weigh that much," she insisted. I suggested she step down and I'd make sure the scale was balanced. She did, and I made a big production of turning the little knob on the side to make sure that the arrow was pointing directly at zero. She could see that it was and she stepped back on. I let Joe, one of the medics, slide the weights back and forth. I stood behind her, leaning backwards, with just

Joe and Chris, medics at the clinic. Their only agenda was to provide good patient care. They made my job easier. When I had to leave for a mission, I had no worries that they would carry on at the clinic.

the toes of my shoe on the scales, which was tricky—keeping my balance and making sure the needle wasn't herky-jerky.

It showed about 140 pounds—probably a few dozen more than she actually weighed—and she was just amazed. "That scale is wrong. I've never weighed that much before," she said.

"You saw it," I said. "We balanced it in front of you. Maybe you just picked up a couple pounds between last month and now."

She said, "I'm eating the same amount, exercising, not doing anything differently."

She was so distressed that we laughed and I broke down and told her what I'd been up to. She looked at me and then laughed too, probably in relief. "I knew I didn't weigh that much," she kept repeating. But she also seemed to enjoy the diversion of the caper. She left the examination room smiling.

Huda had a large cell; nothing like the others. I think she convinced somebody with influence that she suffered from claustropho-

5 ♥

59

HUDA SALIH MAHDI AMMASH
WMD Scientist/
Ba'th Party Regional
Command Member

♠
5

*Huda, who was called Chemical
Sally by our military*

bia. In fact, Colonel Sylvester in effect said as much. This was before
we got there, but it was reported to him that Huda suffered "severe
emotional distress" when kept in an eight-by-ten-foot room. He said
he had been told that she experienced what amounted to seizures in
a normal cell. At least that's what he had been told.

The "group" room she had to herself measured maybe twenty by
forty feet and normally accommodated between twelve and twenty
people, depending on how crowded we wanted to make it. She had
room to do calisthenics and somehow had measured the perimeter to
see how many laps equaled a mile. I don't know how many times she
figured, but every time I passed her cell, she was exercising. She asked
for a treadmill to be sent from home, and I forwarded the request for
her. I later reluctantly took her the answer: "No can do."

I guess I wasn't surprised. When I mentioned it to the security
people, they explained why they couldn't grant Huda this particular
wish, and once they explained how much would be involved it was

pretty clear why. The entire piece of equipment would have had to be disassembled to make sure no contraband—anything either illegal or harmful—was being smuggled in. Then it would need to be reassembled. It was simply too much trouble.

In 1985, Huda was diagnosed with breast cancer, had a radical mastectomy, and apparently had recovered fully. But eight months into our stay at Cropper the rumor of her persistent cancer surfaced, and it was widely circulated in the press that we were holding a woman who was very ill with cancer. To this day I think Tariq Aziz's lawyer, who had been at Cropper the day before the rumor started, leaked the story. We squashed it pretty quickly. First, her handler interviewed her, and she assured him she was healthy, all of which was reported to headquarters.

Just to be on the safe side, we persuaded her to submit to a breast exam by our own Cropper Doc. To ensure her privacy, we covered all the windows and the doors in the clinic and had guards stationed outside the door of the examination room while the exam was going on.

I'm glad to report that Huda was healthy when she was with us, and I'm not sure how it would have worked out if she had not been. We would have liked to have had done more to reassure ourselves and everyone else, but that would have meant taking her to be checked out at the CHS, and she was adamant about not leaving Cropper. There was no persuading her.

She said it would do dishonor to her family if she were to be seen in handcuffs, despite all our assurances that the area would be cleared and she would not be seen by anyone but the staff. No photographs would have been allowed. But she refused, and bowing to her feelings, we didn't force her, as we could have.

She was a nice-looking woman, petite—maybe five feet, two inches at the most—and clear skinned. In fact, she had a flawless olive-toned complexion. Huda wore the traditional robes and scarf, although she didn't cover her face. One day I asked her whether she was hot in all those layers. She said, "Yes, but it's my culture."

Huda spoke very good English, which is not surprising. She had traveled extensively in the United States and had lived here as a little girl. She also attended graduate school in the States. In fact, in addition to her master's degree in microbiology from Texas Women's University in Denton, she had a Ph.D. from the University of Missouri–Columbia. She was married and had four children, and I know she missed her family terribly.

As I mentioned, some details of her incarceration were widely reported in the press, and much of the information was wrong. Besides claiming that she was very ill—some accounts even stated that she was dying—I later read there were claims she was being tortured for information. I can categorically deny that. She was treated very well and with respect.

What I found most remarkable—and what was not widely reported in the press—was that she was nominated for a Nobel Peace Prize while she was in U.S. custody.

Colonel Sylvester said that our unit had handled all the paperwork required by the Nobel Prize committee. "We were responsible for getting her all the materials related to the application, letting her write out the narrative, then transferring it to the next higher headquarters," he explained. "We didn't read it."

Huda's nomination was not widely known, and the only way I learned about it was through Sergeant Major Carpenter. Colonel Sylvester, Carpenter, and Sergeant Major Adams had taken it upon themselves to come up with a plan for handling the ceremony in the event that she emerged as the winner. The plan they developed was to use the courtroom that we had created for the trial of Saddam and his eleven henchmen. In the end it wasn't used that way, but I'll get to that later. For sure, it was the most controlled area in our camp.

Huda didn't win the prize. Talk about a history-making irony if she had: Huda Ammash is honored with a Nobel Peace Prize while in U.S. custody, accused of making weapons of mass destruction.

As Colonel Sylvester said, laughing, "That would have broke the mold."

Although I never found exactly what she was nominated for, I can only guess. Thanks to the Internet, I have been able to learn more about my charges than I ever could have from them directly. Huda, a microbiologist, was obviously highly thought of in her home country, where she had a high post within the Ba'ath Party. In a picture that was widely circulated right before the American invasion, she was shown seated around a table with several male party members, apparently at a meeting, although the significance of that meeting isn't known.

She was a dean and professor at Baghdad University, and her published works and research seem to be centered on documenting the rise of cancers and birth defects in Iraq after the first Gulf War. She centered her studies on depleted uranium that the United States left in great quantities after that war. A radioactive carcinogen used to tip shells and bullets, it can produce particles than can get into lungs, open wounds, water, and the food chain. I have seen estimates that put the amount we left as high as eight hundred tons. Our own military has warned that depleted uranium could cause organ damage, neurocognitive disorders, and several cancers.

At one point I read a speculation that Huda's breast cancer might have been caused by her studies on depleted uranium. But then I looked at the dates and decided against it, unless she was studying this stuff much earlier than the Gulf War. There were nearly ten years between when she was diagnosed with cancer and Desert Storm. Uranium is scary and potent stuff with a very long half-life—four and a half billion years.

Huda was no head-in-the-clouds scientist, either. Politically active, she had been critical of American sanctions on Iraq after her research showed direct links between the environmental hazards after 1991 and the embargo.

As far as the ostensible reason for Huda's detention at Camp

Colonel Sylvester poses below his KU Flag

Cropper—that she had somehow participated in the WMD program—Hans Blix (who lead the UN weapons inspection team that couldn't find any weapons of mass destruction) declined to interview her because he didn't think she was connected with weapons research.

Despite his lack of interest, the next year we put her on our "most wanted" list. I never was sure why she was detained, surely not for sitting at the same table with Saddam Hussein. Apparently, someone somewhere thought we could connect her with WMD, or we could extract information regarding potential WMD. Or maybe we didn't like her criticism of the embargo or her criticism of what we had done to the Iraqi environment. I guess we will never know.

Huda wasn't all about science, exercise, watching her weight, and politics. She obviously had some loyalties to the major university in my home state where she had received her Ph.D. Sergeant Major Adams was also a University of Missouri graduate, and when the colonel, a Jayhawk, put up a University of Kansas flag, Adams wrote home for a Tiger flag for Missouri. He flew it inside the compound, right outside the administration trailer.

One day, Huda noticed it was looking a bit disheveled, which I don't doubt with all that dust swirling around. I'm sure Adams never would have asked her, but she volunteered to wash his Tiger flag. It was near the end of his time there, and he didn't fly it again. He recently reported it is safe, washed, folded, and packed away with his other souvenirs from Iraq.

Huda is somebody I would like to have kept up with. I told her so when I visited her just before we left. She was her stoic self. "Just watch the news," she said. I did. And late in 2005 I heard a very short, one-line item on CNN that she had been released after a joint American-Iraqi board found she was not a security threat after all.

10 | AT THE BAZAAR

W HAT I'M ABOUT TO TELL YOU COULD FALL UNDER ONE OF TWO headings: "bazaar" or "bizarre." There I was, at the bazaar for the purpose of buying cigars for the Ace of Spades. In my mind, that in itself is borderline bizarre.

Weeks before, Vic had mentioned that cigars and a cup of coffee did wonders for his blood pressure. I grant you, this defies conventional medical wisdom, but we were willing to try anything that would put him in a good mood. I passed that on to the general, the head of detainee operations, who was then visiting Camp Cropper. He came every two weeks to make sure things were going well with Saddam. He didn't usually visit him; he just talked to me and the doctor in charge.

A move to new quarters at North Victory was in the offing, and it seemed imperative that Saddam be in topnotch shape for this. The general got me and the doctor together one day in July to discuss the plans—plans that Saddam was in the dark about. They didn't tell us why the move was being considered. We figured because it was closer to the building that had been turned into a courthouse for the purpose of trying Saddam and his eleven co-conspirators. At this point, plans for the use of the 439th courtroom at Camp Cropper for this purpose, had been scuttled.

I guess they rationalized that it was less of a security risk to have Saddam being incarcerated closer to the courtroom, but I think they were wrong. My own opinion is that the security was better at Cropper. Also at Cropper all the high Muckity Mucks would have a harder time getting in, and they all wanted to see the great theater that the trial would present. But no one asked me.

When I mentioned the bit about the cigars and coffee, the general said, "Tune him up." That meant lower his blood pressure plus get him in a better frame of mind for the move. So we knew that we had implicit permission to buy cigars for Vic. We also knew we would be spending more time with him in a social sense as we worked to get him in the best state of mind as possible. Once again, I was struck by the irony: all this work to keep Saddam Hussein in top-notch shape, both medically and psychologically, so he could go to the gallows a healthy man.

Al-Faw Palace, one of Saddam's domiciles. He commissioned it to commemorate Iraq's re-taking of the Al-Faw Peninsula during the Iran-Iraq War. We went there for our demobilization briefings.

Sergeant Major Adams in Al-Faw Palace.

But I shrugged and soldiered on, and I added cigars to the list of stuff to buy at our next trip to the bazaar, where I usually went once every two or three weeks.

The bazaar, which was next to the Post-Exchange, otherwise known as the PX, was like a gypsy caravan with different vendors all under one huge tent. There was only one way in and one way out. The floor was sandy, and most of it was covered by beautifully patterned rugs. I can shut my eyes and smell the incense to this day.

It was dusty and musky and well-lit thanks to generators the size of large pickup trucks.

You could buy just about anything there: perfume, watches, clothing, jewelry, knives, swords, rugs, walkie talkies, cell phones, musical instruments, and coffee. There was always a steady stream of customers. I'm sure the location next to the department-store-like PX was deliberate, and they drew customers from each other.

There were things in the bazaar that you didn't find in the PX or, for that matter, anywhere else. Somebody had set up a photo booth where you could have your picture taken in Arab garb—simple black robe with a full-length gold stripe and headdress. I never did that, but one time I bought a *dishdasha*, robe, and headdress, paying a few dollars extra to get Egyptian cotton—"the finest Eqyptian cotton" the lady said—rather than polyester. Now that I'm home with it, I can't seem to find many opportunities to wear it. I suspect I'd get lots of impolite stares if I showed up wearing it for Monday night line dancing or Thursday night Latin dancing. I think it would probably not work well at 24-Hour Fitness, where I go every day when I'm not working. My silly purchase is now gathering dust in my closet at home. Maybe I'll go out dressed as Saddam Hussein on Halloween.

One day with Valentine's Day approaching, I decided to make a Valentine card for Rita. I put on just the headdress and wore only some boxer shorts covered with hearts that Rita had given me. They worked well for the card, which read on the front, "Who loves you, baby?" I probably exposed a bit too much of myself in the picture that our librarian—Citrus 4—took on his digital camera, but I figured hell, only Rita would be seeing it.

Some of the guys bought rugs to send back home. I didn't buy any rugs, but I always bought incense and I brought a bunch home. It came in scents I'd never seen or smelled. One smelled like ripe bananas. Another was called "Eyes."

There is something very exotic and sensual about those Arab women who only show their eyes when they go out. Many wore just enough eye makeup to be noticeable, and I must say when they returned my gaze it was captivating. Maybe I was fantasizing about the desire I thought I saw in those eyes. Maybe it had been too long since I'd seen Rita. I suspect that feeling is not as unusual as we Americans like to think and some smart marketing person picked up on that when it came to naming an incense.

A package of incense would last a long time, and I used it in my room at Camp Cropper. Some of the guys didn't like it though and complained about it when they came to my room. I burned it partly because I liked it and partly to get rid of some of the bad smells that persisted in the heat and humidity. Earlier in my stay, we had no toilets or running water, and we were all in one big room. I was always self-conscious about what I imagined was an occasional urine smell, and I worried that maybe I missed when I urinated into a bottle in the middle of the night. (Who wanted to get dressed in the middle of the night to go to those awful Porta Johns?) I was religious about keeping those bottles emptied and washed out, but I burned incense just in case.

The bazaar was also loud—just like in the movies—with all the haggling going on. There was always some guy wanting to be my new best friend, waiting to pounce: "Buddy, buddy, where you from? U.S.? I've been to the United States. My cousin lives in Iowa. I make you good deal on a Rolex watch. Gold bracelet you want? We have the finest gold in the world." They were everywhere, every few steps.

On this particular day, we weren't easily distracted. We were on a mission to buy cigars for Saddam Hussein. I'm sure the irony also struck my partner in crime, Cropper Doc. I really liked this particular doctor, who had been with us maybe a couple months by this time. He was a family practitioner and very athletic—played softball, basketball, and even boxed. I saw him working out on the heavy bag in the gym once. Maybe he felt these were skills he needed to hone. I also have a picture of him climbing a tree. Plus, he knew something about cigars. I knew nothing.

"I'm not buying Montecristos for that guy," he said. (We were spending our own money, by the way. I'm sure we could have asked for funds, but we never thought about it. I'm glad now, because I can assure the American taxpayers they weren't buying Saddam Hussein cigars.) Anyway, we settled on Cohibas, which come either from Cuba or the Dominican Republic.

When we came back to the camp, we took the cigars to Saddam during his evening rec time. He was pleased and surprised and invited us to join him, so we each grabbed a chair and sat outside in the recreation yard. It was about 8 p.m. during his twice-daily rec time. The stars were coming out and I seem to recall moonlight. It was pleasant at any rate.

I'd never smoked a cigar, and Saddam took it upon himself to teach me. "Don't inhale," he told me, and I didn't. It was okay. These cigars were mild, and they tasted pretty good.

He seldom smoked an entire cigar. He'd get halfway through and stop, saying, "Save for later." Sometimes he'd just wave the cigar in front of his nose and just savor the aroma of the half-smoked cigar. I considered this to be an example of both his frugality and good coping skills, making do with a partly smoked cigar.

He couldn't smoke by himself because he didn't have matches. But, that aside, I think he really did prefer for us to join him in what seemed to be a very social ritual for him. He always liked to drink coffee with his cigar.

For reasons I can't understand, it really did seem to lower his blood pressure. He didn't always have coffee available, but he usually had some Folgers packets of instant coffee on hand. So, in the absence of a steaming cup of coffee, he would open up one of the packets, empty it into the cup, pour cold water into it, and stir it with his finger. "What we do," he'd say. And then he'd smile while sipping his cold coffee. I'm no coffee drinker, but the very thought of that cold instant stuff makes me shudder, but I just chalked this up to another example of Vic's good coping skills.

So here we were, Saddam Hussein, Cropper Doc, George Piro at times, and me, smoking cigars and male bonding whether we wanted to or not. I can tell you that on the nights we turned up to smoke with him, he was always very happy.

We never smoked inside, and when we'd show up with the cigars, he'd stand up, shake our hands, and then lead the way outside. I found it rather touching, the way he maintained the façade of being in charge and welcoming his guests. Maybe it was his habit to treat guests—the ones he liked—that way. Maybe for a brief moment he tried to make himself forget where he was. Maybe for a brief moment he *did* forget where he was. Regardless, he was always polite and hospitable. We did this two or three times a week, and it turned out to be a rather pleasant interlude for all of us.

But I'm not in the habit of deceiving people, and when I thought about it, I was uncomfortable knowing this was part of a much bigger and secret plan to move Vic to his new quarters, and, in the even bigger picture, to return him to Iraqi custody to seal his fate.

My own personal conflict would not subside.

The cigars were a welcome break, I'm sure, but Saddam seemed to occupy himself very well day in and day out, reading, writing, and praying, which he did five times a day. I didn't interrupt if I happened to be making rounds while he was praying. The prayers didn't last long. I'd usually give him ten minutes and then go back.

Saddam didn't have a watch, but he shouldn't have needed one to figure out when to pray. He could certainly have heard when the calls came from the nearest mosque, which was a few miles away. But frequently he wanted to know the time. Once, when he asked me the time, I took off my own watch and gave it to him. I figured I could get another one easily enough, and many of the other detainees had their own watches. But the word got out, and the word came down that I couldn't do this, so I had to ask old Vic for my watch back.

I learned later that the watch was a big part of George's method of manipulating Saddam during the interrogation. George not only wore a big watch, but he also made sure than none of the guards around Saddam had a watch. That way, George would—in a psychological sense—control Saddam's time. Clever, but I didn't know about this ruse until much later.

Vic was also an avid reader, and he read his Quran daily. You can tell he really liked to read, and he wasn't just reading to kill time. He even had books with him when they captured him in that hole near Tikrit.

Occasionally, he'd ask for a specific book. To my surprise, he once asked for a book about Judaism. For some reason, he wanted to learn more about Jewish people. He also asked for a Bible in Arabic. Those requests went through me to our librarian; I never learned whether he was able to honor those requests.

I wish I had more information about this. We never discussed anything about Judaism or Israel. Ever. We weren't supposed to get into anything that might be controversial. But later, in a short little book called *Saddam Hussein*, by Dale Anderson, I read a most interesting anecdote.

Anderson writes mostly for young people, but this book leaves little to the imagination about Saddam's tyranny. Presumably to address the very issue of the complexity and the coexistence of good and evil that I've been grappling with, he tells the story of what happened to an Iraqi Jew named Na'im Tawina.

It seems that Tawina was falsely accused in the early 1970s of spying for Israel. Such a charge usually brought a penalty of death, and he had little hope of leaving prison alive. One day he was taken to a torture room, but just before the torture began, Saddam entered the room and gave orders to the guards to forget the torture and to release Tawina. "He is a good man. I know him," Saddam was quoted as saying.

Tawina didn't understand, but he certainly wasn't going to argue. Years later, after leaving Iraq for Israel, he saw a photograph of Saddam as a child, and all became clear. Among his several childhood "occupations," Saddam had sold cigarettes. Tawina recognized the child and remembered buying cigarettes from the boy. He also remembered tipping the child well. "Hussein remembered his kindness and repaid the man with his life," Anderson concludes.

I saw a quote from Saddam's writings about the threat from the Shia in Iran being greater than the threat from Israel: "The spread of the Persians . . . is more dangerous for Iraq than the Zionist entity, now and in the future. The Persians are summarily dangerous to the Arab nation, especially the Arab countries of the Gulf."

Reading, writing, and praying was pretty much how he spent his days except for the outdoors time in his rec area, which, unless we were smoking, was about forty-five minutes. Once he mentioned that he was having some problems seeing to read and write in the dim light of his cell. I reported this, and we decided to have an Army optometrist check his eyes. I remember how he brought in all his fancy equipment, and we carried it back to the wood. I had the distinct feeling the optometrist was a little apprehensive in the beginning; once he got going, I think he was fine.

Vic got some new glasses. I remember he put them on, picked up some papers as if to test them, took them off again, then put them back on. He nodded his head in approval and smiled. No more squinting.

Meanwhile, I took it upon myself to get him a brighter light, because I'd noticed the light in his cell was quite dim. I installed a bulb that had a higher wattage.

With an apologetic chuckle to the FBI, I must mention an unintended consequence of the new 100-watt bulb. After I installed the new light bulb, the extra heat melted the support for a small camera that was hidden in the ceiling fixture, and it fell down inside the round globe that covered the bulb. When I say small, I mean small. It looked sort of like a miniature domino when it was up in that light fixture. I'd seen it when I installed the bulb and, frankly, wasn't sure what it was.

Vic didn't miss much, and I'm pretty sure he knew his room was bugged. But he just pointed to the fixture and asked what had fallen down in there. Then it dawned on me, but I played dumb. The next time he was in the rec area we gave him some extra time, and another FBI agent came in with a ladder and quickly installed a new camera. And we cut back a little on the wattage, probably to a 75-watt bulb that wasn't so hot.

These bugs don't like the heat.

11 | THE TRIAL BEGINS

IT WAS JUNE 30, 2004. AT HOME, PEOPLE WERE BUYING FIREWORKS, planning their barbecues, preparing for the long 4th of July weekend. It was hot there, and it was hot here. And sunny. The sun was always shining in Iraq it seemed. The few times it rained was just enough to move the dirt around.

It was also the first day of Vic's court appearances. He was in court all day. When I went to see him in the evening, he was putting on a pretty good front as he tried to appear upbeat, but I could tell he was somewhat down. He seemed tired, and when I asked him how he felt, he said the trial was taxing, or words to that effect.

In court, he looked dapper, though. Handsome actually. Our supply sergeant, Greg Seavey, had made a request for special funds for buying suits for all the detainees who were going on trial. Suits, white shirts, and nice shoes. No ties.

Although the Interim Iraqi Government went into effect at the end of June, the United States retained physical custody of all the detainees, and since they were still in our custody, they were supposed to look good. Seavey told me recently that he spent two weeks getting all the right sizes for the twelve defendants. He also recalled that Saddam didn't like the way the first suit fit so Greg was able to exchange it with the suit of his half brother, Barzan al-Tikriti. Saddam's original suit was tan. The one he ended up with was a Christian Dior—a knockoff actually.

And that's not the half of it. They were fitted out with Oakley sunglasses that were the envy of all the guards. But they, too, must have been knockoffs. Seavey remembers the paperwork from the effort: five hundred dollars for outfitting all twelve detainees in new suits, belts, shirts, shoes, and socks. The contract for one hundred pairs of sunglasses was for thirty-five dollars, and the logos included Oakley, RayBan, and Nike. This was accomplished with help from the International Committee for the Red Cross (ICRC). I'm thinking of appointing Greg my personal shopper.

The court proceeding that first day lasted much longer than any of us anticipated. It was held at North Victory, about five miles from Camp Cropper. Sometime in the late afternoon I got worried. I'd expected everybody back by now. So many of my charges were on a treatment regimen, and it was time for their medications. At least four were diabetic, and I figured they were long overdue for insulin. A diabetic can't properly process food without it. I felt I couldn't wait any longer, so I called Colonel Sylvester on his two-way radio to get directions for the exact location of the court proceedings, and then I drove over to North Victory. But first I went back to the clinic to get their various medications, insulin, and syringes and labeled everything carefully. I stuck it all in my pockets.

True Story and Saber 9 (Carpenter and Adams) and some 89th military police had been at North Victory all day. They'd been waiting on the Rhino Bus—a heavily armored vehicle that can hold as many as thirty passengers. I went inside and tried to find the courtroom. Then I found someone to get all the detainees who needed medication out of the courtroom. There was another glitch when we discovered that the numbers we'd assigned to each detainee did not correspond with the list that had been provided to the Interim Iraqi Government by one of the many U.S. agencies involved. Eventually, this got sorted out and I was able to start laying out both insulin and the various oral meds in a room just outside the courtroom.

But I was stopped by none other than Chemical Ali, whom I had sent for, along with a few others. When he saw me laying out the insulin he held up his hand. "No," he said. "No need for medicine. I have not eaten." His intervention was a good thing. Insulin on an empty stomach would probably have sent him into insulin shock. But the issue still remained that they'd been kept there all day since early morning without food or water.

I was upset, and I suspect I showed it. I asked to speak to whoever was in charge. A captain with the 89th military police brigade was summoned and, to my surprise, he admitted culpability. They were so busy dealing with all the legalities and the logistics, he said, that they forgot that people needed to eat.

As we watched our charges when they returned to Camp Cropper, we all felt pretty good. It made us realize that we weren't doing such a bad job in our caretaking capacity. They had all been pretty dejected when they started out in the morning. Chemical Ali, for instance, looking like he was at death's door, appeared to be barely able to get up the steps into the bus. Returning, he practically bounded down those same steps.

They were all so, so happy to be back, they were hugging everyone in sight. We suspected that morning they were thinking they might never see the light of day again. "They were happy to be with us because every day they were with us was one more day they were alive," Adams observed. But back at North Victory, they had not wanted to get off the bus, much less go in the courtroom, Adams and the colonel later reported. Colonel Sylvester was in the court's holding room with them when their handcuffs were taken off.

Because the Iraqis were so adamant about keeping an Iraqi face on the proceedings, none of our guys could show their faces. But Colonel Sylvester's hand might have shown up in some pictures as

Chemical Ali coming to his arraignment.

he shoved Chemical Ali, who, dazed and shackled, was apparently reluctant to go any further into the courtroom. To say they were loathe to face their accusers is putting it mildly. And, as Adams reminded us, they knew more about Iraqi justice than we did.

Some time later, Colonel Sylvester told me about how—at the end of that day's proceedings—he happened to see two Iraqi guards trying to crush Chemical Ali's wrist as they put his handcuffs back on. He learned later that they might have been exacting a little retribution. According to his sources, the cousin of one of guards had been shot in the head, and the other guard had been beaten by Chemical Ali.

The status of some of my charges changed after this court date. Once they had been formally charged with a crime, they were now considered "high value criminal detainees," and on July 1 they were

Supply Sergeant Greg Seavey.

moved to a separate part of the compound that we called the Green Mile. We got that from the movie by the same title with Tom Hanks. A chain-link fence kept them completely segregated.

For some reason, everyone's tensions seemed to be heightened at that time. Getting the detainees back and forth to the trial added to our hours and our duties. Plus, I couldn't help but wonder if we weren't absorbing some of our charges' anxiety. We also might have been feeling more testy than usual because of the extreme heat. I think that month the thermometer registered at least 130 degrees F. At 100 degrees it was actually bearable, and we welcomed those days. "It gets down to 100 and you start looking for a coat," said the ever-witty Adams. Sometimes at night it was actually quite comfortable. The first couple months we were there it could get quite cool at night. The desert was a strange place, and there was a huge disparity between night and day. Some early mornings you could actually see your breath. But when the sun came out, it heated up real quick.

Somebody asked me recently to describe exactly *how* hot it was, and the best example I could come up with was that it was so hot we tried to re-train our bowels so we could perform that daily function during the night hours in order to avoid using the Porta Johns during the daytime. Those black plastic seats would burn your butt; in fact, you couldn't sit on them at certain hours. That's how hot it was. We'd put off going until it simply couldn't be put off. You could always tell when you saw someone sprinting towards the sallyport that the inevitable could be put off no longer. You knew he had waited until the last minute to get to the closest Porta Johns, which were located just outside the compound about fifty yards away.

While I'm on the subject of Porta Johns, they were pumped out regularly by an Iraqi contractor who one day reported finding something other than the usual contents that need no further description. It seems that departing units on their way back to the States would relieve themselves in more ways than one in our Porta

Porta Johns and guard tower outside the compound.

Johns. Hand grenades and other unused ammunition, for instance, that they weren't supposed to have and that would not have cleared customs, were disposed of in our toilets. Hand grenades are small and are easily clipped to your belt, so they were no big deal to carry. The soldiers could have turned them in no questions asked, but they probably didn't know that. Better to get rid of them before, I guess they were thinking. Can you imagine the mess if one had exploded? When someone was using the toilet? I can't, and it's highly unlikely anyway. As long as the pin is in the grenade, it's theoretically safe, but it still pains me to contemplate.

Some time around May we had been moved to new quarters at Camp Cropper where we had indoor plumbing. We felt we were in the lap of luxury. Before the end of the summer, I had a room with a bathroom *and* a shower that I shared with one other person. In a little lobby nearby, we had a television and somehow procured some chairs the 112th had left behind.

Leather chairs left by the 112th

On July 22, I wrote:

It's been a busy month. I'm starting to feel the pressure. Blood draw today for labs at 0600, will miss breakfast; #52 to CSH at 0900 for tooth abscess and cyst on eye . . . and it's hot outside!

After the aforementioned blood draw, Joe, one of the medics from the 118th who was always with me in the clinic, and the crew put the tubes on ice while I went to my room and armed myself for the trip to the CHS. "Another day in the life of Ellis," I said to myself. I felt as if my teeth were clenching and that my life was a series of going from one crisis to the next. But, I told myself, that's the life of a soldier and I really was not complaining, knowing what some of my fellow soldiers were going through—out there in the desert or on foot patrols in the streets in Baghdad.

I noticed they were putting No. 52 in the third vehicle with the MPs, and I was riding in the second. I would have preferred to be in the same vehicle with my patients, but that seldom happened. We left Camp Cropper at 9 a.m. in four gun trucks with all of us in radio contact. The windows were down, and although it was dusty it was good to breathe a little fresh air, because once we got to Route Irish, the windows went up and we were locked and loaded, with the pedal to the metal, and we didn't stop until we reached the CHS.

Passing under highway overpasses were particularly problematic, and we always criss-crossed so that we didn't come out from under the overpass in the same position that we entered. The reason for this was so the bad guys couldn't be in position to drop a grenade into the hole in our vehicle where the turret gunner stands, thus blowing us up.

I scanned my sector, and the other three people in the vehicle were doing the same; everybody had a job. No one was talking as we *tried* to remain calm. We were all tense, watching every vehicle, building, and pedestrian. Traffic started to slow down as we got near the

CSH. Suddenly, we heard shots. Push that car out of the way, keep going, don't stop, keep going, keep going, keep going. Incoming RPG. You can see those coming. This one landed somewhere near but not on us. Shit. Keep going. Anyone hurt? Convoy commander: all vehicles report. Nobody hurt. Exhale.

We reached the CSH to find a big, gaping hole in the highway. Must have been a hellava car bomb—or, in militarese, a VBIED, or vehicle-borne improvised explosive device. This place looked like a scene from *Mad Max*: remnants of cars all over the place. I saw bloodstains on the ground but no injured people.

There was a tank sitting near the entrance to the CSH, which was a good sign. No one was coming through here. We breathed a sigh of relief. It was probably a false sense of security inside the CSH, but at least you were inside a concrete building—better than out on the street.

By I p.m., No. 52 had been seen, we checked the status of Route Irish for our return trip, and, wonder of wonders, it was all clear. So we mounted up, locked and loaded, and headed for home, a trip that turned out to be uneventful. I breathed a few deep breaths, secured my weapons in my room, and returned to the clinic to check on things and to make my report.

I only had a couple of cookies to sustain me all day, and I sure was ready for dinner. I also was ready for this day to end, but first I made my evening check on Saddam. It was 8 p.m., and as I went to the wood I managed a couple of jokes with the guards before I got to Vic, who rose from his cot where he'd been sitting, greeted me with his customary handshake and offer of a chair, which I fell into happily.

"I had my shirt off when I hear you come and I get dressed fast," he said. Then he picked up his writing tablet and started to read what he'd written. As usual, he read what he'd written in Arabic, then, using hand gestures and his rapidly improving English, he'd try to explain it.

When he'd get to something that was really complicated or that he couldn't explain, he'd say, "We'll wait for George." When George was there, he'd give us a running interpretation. Sometimes he'd have to consult a little book that he kept in his pocket. It was probably a pocket dictionary.

But this time, on July 22, the day after George had left Camp Cropper, he was clearly on Vic's mind. "This is for George," he said.

After he finished, a tear—a single tear—slid down his cheek. His sadness showed on every feature of his face. I bet I'm one of the few to ever see the adult Saddam Hussein cry.

I rather felt his pain. George, as I have already discussed, was there to interrogate Saddam, not to be his friend. But by becoming his friend, he was a more effective interrogator. Saddam was missing his friend, not his interrogator.

I'm well aware of Saddam's image as a vicious thug and nothing more, but I found him charismatic, sometimes charming and often funny, and I think others who worked with him felt the same way. I also know that the differences in our two cultures represent such a chasm that I should—and did—reserve judgment.

I know about his hunger for power and rumors of his paranoia. I know how, shortly after he assumed power by forcing out the man who had been his mentor and protector, President Ahmed Hassan al-Bakr, he then proceeded to execute several leaders of the Ba'ath Party whom he considered to be disloyal.

Then, after the purge, he set out to show himself to be a man of the people. Lest there be any doubt, he had larger-than-life pictures of himself put everywhere. Some showed him in military uniform, some in a business suit, some in traditional Arab dress. A joke circulated that Saddam Hussein's pictures were roughly equivalent to the male population in Iraq.

At the same time that he was executing his political rivals and dreaming of Arab unification, he had also started to implement some of his big ideas. And good ideas they were. He began the process of modernizing the Iraqi economy and, thanks to increasing oil revenues, he was able to increase spending on schools, hospitals, and clinics.

In 1982, he won a UNESCO (United Nations Educational, Scientific and Cultural Organization) award for a literacy project called the National Campaign for the Eradication of Illiteracy and the Implementation of Compulsory Free Education in Iraq. With regard to the "compulsory" component, I'd read somewhere that the punishment for not attending literacy classes was three years in prison, but I certainly don't know if that's true. If it *is* true, I'd say that's definitely a "Godfather"-like incentive.

I have read that social services that the Ba'athist government provided were unheard of in many Middle Eastern countries: free hospitalization was granted to everyone, families of soldiers killed in war were supported, and farmers were given subsidies after land was redistributed to the peasants. The status of women was vastly improved, and they became an important part of the workforce.

Granted that Saddam's motives might not have been completely pure, that all this was to keep people in line, that he ran a regime of fear and distrust, I still don't think most people are aware of some of the good things he did. With the nationalization of oil fields and refineries, electricity was available to almost everyone in Iraq, even some in remote villages. The government built roads and promoted mining and other industries to diversify the previously oil-dependent economy. Saddam also introduced Western-style banking while simultaneously providing traditional Arab banking, to give Iraqis a choice. (The Western style offered interest-bearing accounts, which the Arab style did not.)

The flip side was the aforementioned fear that people lived under. And, of course, Saddam involved Iraq in a protracted war against Iran that left his country bankrupt and unable to pay the massive loans from Kuwait and Saudi Arabia in particular. He seemed especially incensed that, while he had been fighting, those countries had been growing increasingly wealthy.

He asked that those debts be forgiven, and he even asked for $30 billion more. Then came the ill-fated (for him) invasion of Kuwait, because the United States got involved swiftly and decisively in Operation Desert Storm; then the embargo, which turned out to be disastrous for the Iraqi people; all the brouhaha about the weapons inspections and his refusal to comply with the UN; and the failed "oil for food" program, in which he was accused of selling the food and using the money for weapons.

For more than twenty years, Saddam pretty much held absolute power, and, according to the cliché, that's supposed to corrupt absolutely. I don't doubt that he was corrupted and corrupt. For sure he had—and took—too much power. On the other hand, I often wonder how I would handle such power.

I can only assume that some of this made it into his writing, which continued at an almost feverish pace. At some point he had written so much he obviously needed to get his papers in order. He apparently determined that he needed a hole punch, but he didn't know the correct word. He showed me the stack of papers and then pantomimed punching a hole in them. "Oh," I said, "a hole punch." He nodded, obviously pleased. I lost track after that. Either somebody got him a hole punch or punched it for him, after which he strung some string through the holes and tied it, holding the pages together and making his own very crude book. He was more than satisfied. Happy really. He held up the strung-together papers with a gesture of total satisfaction.

He wrote sitting on his cot, his back against the wall. It was a very narrow and low cot, so his feet touched the floor as if he were sitting on a bench. The writing—always in Arabic and on yellow legal pads that we provided along with pencils—seemed to have become the most compelling part of his existence.

At the same time, he seemed to be working to improve his spoken

English. Often, he'd ask me how to spell a word and sometimes use gestures in order to get the correct word to express himself. Then he'd make sure to use that word in a sentence the next time I saw him. But the simplest things could hang him up. Once he was grappling for the word *little*. He used hand gestures, his hands getting closer and closer, then finally he showed a small space between his thumb and index finger. The word he was grasping for seemed so obvious I didn't think of it at first. "Oh, you mean *little*, I said," and he nodded emphatically. Considering the circumstances, I found it rather touching that Vic was so determined to continue learning.

On this particular evening, Saddam seemed to want to talk, and for some reason he wanted to talk about Al Qaeda. He reiterated that he never aligned with Bin Laden. "Advisors say align with Bin Laden; America will think you with Bin Laden anyway. I say no align with Bin Laden and sign papers that say no align with Bin Laden," he said, making a sweeping gesture with his hand. I so wanted to ask him more, but then I remembered that was not my job.

I headed back to my room for a shower, some music, and a movie on my little portable DVD player. That night I somehow felt a strong need to clear my head. I have often thought it is good we don't know what's coming. We are so much better off being ignorant of the future and so much better able to do our jobs in the present.

I slept a dreamless sleep that night. Mercifully dreamless.

12 | THIS TIME IT'S LARRY

I HAD NO IDEA WHAT WAS COMING WHEN I GOT A CALL ON MY TWO-way radio late in the morning on August 5. It just said to report to the White Trailer, the administration headquarters and place where prisoners were processed. I was smoking cigars with Vic, and I cut my visit short.

When I got to the White Trailer, Jayhawker, the colonel, was waiting outside. He handed me two notes, one saying to call Rita about my brother and another to call the Red Cross.

I knew this couldn't be good. I called Rita, and she told me my brother Larry was bleeding from his esophagus and had been given five units of blood. His blood pressure was 80 over 20 and his hemoglobin was 6 grams per deciliter. He was on a dopamine drip, which is what they use to get blood going to the vital organs. They'd stopped the bleeding once, but it had started up again. When I heard those numbers I knew that my brother was dying, that he was bleeding to death.

I felt as if my whole body was no longer rigid, as if my bones had suddenly turned into something soft and squishy. My head probably slumped forward, and I felt I needed to use extra control to keep the rest of my body from following. The only thing that felt

A photo of our extended family. From left, our mother, Lola Foster; my sister, Beverly; Larry; Me; and my nephew, Jonathon. In front are my nieces, Sylvia Foster and Marilyn Foster, daughters of my sister, Bertha, who died shortly after we moved from Pruitt-Igoe.

rigid was the tightness in my throat. The colonel stood there while I was reading the messages, and he knew what was going on. He was sympathetic although he didn't say much. What he said was, "Get your stuff, and I'll get you a ride to the APOD." I went back to my room to pack my bags, thinking, "Here we go again." I remember looking up toward the sky wanting to shake my fist at whatever it is we call God. I resisted that urge.

I was also thinking that God must have an unrealistic notion of my strength, because I've heard again and again that God never gives you any more than you can handle. I wonder who thought that one up. Seems to me like a good way to keep folks in line: "God did this so I must prove I'm strong enough to handle it."

It was a hot day in Iraq, easily 130 degrees F, and six months to the very day since my mother had died. Outside, it was so hot I felt like I was standing next to a burning building. The heat bore down on me as I moved zombie-like through the compound, but for some reason I was remembering a typical St. Louis summer day, which was hot too. Maybe it was not as hot as Iraq, but the projects seemed to hold the heat better than other places in St. Louis, infamous for its heat and humidity. I'm thinking of all those massive brick buildings absorbing all that heat and not a breath of air stirring among them. At Pruitt-Igoe as a child, we had one fan in our little apartment, and we'd often lie on a pallet on the floor in front of the old oscillating fan.

Despite the chores our mother left us with, we had plenty of down time in the summer to just hang out with friends. We were sort of urban Huck Finns, and we got into plenty of mischief in the rough and tumble projects.

Larry was a cute, pudgy little kid with a round face and dimpled cheeks. But even as a little boy, he was a mischief-maker. Once, he found some matches and he and a little girl from down the hall set some curtains in our apartment on fire. I think one of my sisters put out the fire and that was the end of it, except for the whipping I'm sure he got for that little escapade.

He lost his dimples when he grew older. His hair was short even during those 1960s years. We were never allowed to have Afros, even when they were the fashion of the day. Whenever our hair got more than a centimeter long, my mother would cut it. I've kept my hair short ever since.

Something about hot, dusty days always reminds me of Larry and how he and I and the other kids loved to play mumbly peg, one of our favorite summertime games. If you're old enough you probably remember the game; I wonder if kids today play it. It's probably considered too dangerous. We used ice picks or screwdrivers or knives—screwdrivers worked the best—to do a series of maneuvers that ended up with the tip of whatever we were using sticking more or less upright in the dirt.

The maneuvers had names—Mama, Chicago, Baby, and Papa—and increasing degrees of difficulty. You might start holding the blade and you'd flip it and make it stick in the dirt. Or you might hold the handle and flip it, or throw it over your wrist. Another, Scratch the Match, meant you put the blade in the palm of your hand and flipped it from there. The final, Spank Out, meant you held the tool sideways, then dropped it, hitting the handle to make it stick in the dirt.

The most talented players went through all the maneuvers quickly. The loser was the one left struggling to finish. Once, when a guy we called "Boone" overshot the little circle of soft dirt we'd made for the game, the ice pick buried itself in the top of a little girl's foot. To this day, I remember the criss-crossed sandals she was wearing and how the pick just missed one of the straps of leather. We all sort of froze and then Boone pulled out the pick. Boy did the blood spurt then, but as far as I can remember, she never screamed or even cried. Two of us carried her to May Peeples, one of the mothers who lived close by on the first floor. Mrs. Peeples washed the wound and got the bleeding stopped.

Yes, girls played these games too. Some girls were just as rough and tough as the boys. At the end of our mumbly peg game, we'd bury the tool and the loser would have to "root the peg," meaning he'd have to uncover the tool with his chin, then pull it out with his teeth. No small feat because we'd stomp it into the ground and cover it up with dirt. I shudder to think how filthy we must have gotten ourselves. To my knowledge, nobody broke a tooth, but we must have eaten dirt; we couldn't help it.

Obviously we didn't worry much about germs then. Sometimes, when it got so hot even kids could hardly stand it, we'd all walk down to the riverfront and swim in the Mississippi River, which was probably even dirtier than it is now. It was about two miles away.

If you know anything about America's major river, you know it's muddy and full of strange eddies and dangerous currents. We didn't even know we were doing anything especially dangerous. It just felt good. I can tell you my poor hardworking mother didn't know what we were doing. She wasn't very happy to find us so dirty, I can tell you.

* * *

I WAS JARRED BACK TO THE PRESENT WHEN TRUE STORY, WHO had been recruited to drive me, appeared in the tactical operations center, or TOC, where I'd gone to call the Red Cross. "Seems like all I do is take you to the airport," he said, good-naturedly. And then I remembered that he also was my chauffer to the airport when my mother died six months ago.

I also remembered what he had said to me on our first trip to the airport. "This may seem harsh," he had said, "but you have to put your feelings aside in order to carry on your mission and keep yourself from being killed." Ironically, True Story himself had a bit of a close call on our second trip. I didn't know it until afterward, but the very spot where he had parked as we waited for the plane was hit by a rocket shortly after he pulled away. Good thing my plane was on time.

Soon, I was on the C-130 for Kuwait, and for a while I didn't have to worry about any of my responsibilities. I was in someone else's hands, and I tried to close my eyes and let go of everything for a while. It was about an hour and a half flight, which was more than enough time in that uncomfortable cargo plane. We were strapped into seats that were sort of like canvas benches along the walls of the plane's interior. My knees were almost touching the person across from me, and there was no space to straighten my legs. It was also extremely hot, and the noise from the propellers made conversation difficult—not that I wanted to talk. No one talked.

I couldn't push the sadness away. I still wasn't used to knowing that my mother wasn't back in St. Louis waiting for my call, and now I was going through these same emotions again. I simply wasn't ready for this.

At Camp Wolverine in Kuwait, I went to the PX and bought some clothes. They had changed the requirements for military personnel who were flying. You had to have civilian clothes, so I bought some pants and a shirt but kept on my boots.

There's a big room at Camp Wolverine for military folks, and I was able to grab a cot and lie there and wait for instructions about when the bus would be available to take me to the airport. I was feeling very alone, trying to make my way through this strange place by myself.

I was also feeling something else, and that was anger. I was angry at my little brother, who, shall we say, chose a different lifestyle from mine. It was self-destructive to say the least. He was into drugs, alcohol, and pimping. And he started early with his con work. Once, when he was in his teens, Mom got a call from somebody who said he'd kidnapped Larry and wanted money to free him. In the background you can hear Larry saying, "Oh, oh, oh," like he's being hurt. I heard her cry, "Don't hurt him," and then, "Okay."

Fifteen minutes, later Larry was coming down the street, some rope dangling from his wrist and some sort of handkerchief around his neck like he'd been blindfolded. He said they'd let him go so he could get money for his own release. Yeah, right. But Mom fell for it. I don't know how much she gave him, but I know he used it for drugs.

Larry was fifty-two when he died, but he was lucky he made it that far. You can only abuse your body for so long. For years, he'd had all sorts of health problems, most of them lifestyle induced—cirrhosis of the liver, for instance.

One time, I picked him up at a drugstore in University City, an inner suburb of St. Louis. He had his prescription drugs in one hand and a pint of Jack Daniels Black in the other. He got in the car, put the pills on the dashboard, pulled out a glass from his pocket, then grabbed a handful of pills. I said, "What the hell are you doing?"

He said, "I'm taking my medicine."

I said, "Man there's no medicine in the world gonna work when you taking it like that."

He had a gift of gab and could talk the talk. He also had a lot of women in his time. He survived being stabbed at the age of eighteen and shot in his early twenties. He did time in prison when he was in his thirties and living in California. I guess the conviction was drug-related, but I don't really know. But, wouldn't you know, he also found Jesus in prison. I don't mean to sound cynical. Anything that would get him back on track was fine with me. Eventually, he returned to St. Louis, got a job, went to church every Sunday, and tried to put his life in order.

Most of this effort was too late, at least for this time around. He could barely walk down the steps without falling. By then, he was in a nursing home, and I was always on them to adjust the dosage of his medication. I think he was over-medicated. He was self-medicating with insulin, and I'd be willing to bet he put himself into a diabetic coma. Once, he had been on the floor of his apartment for maybe eighteen hours before his girlfriend, Debra, and my sister, Dorothy, found him. He was unconscious and stayed in a coma for a couple of weeks.

It was all downhill after that. I still don't know exactly how he died, but now it really doesn't matter. I thought of how many times he resolved to get his act together, how he kept finding Jesus, but then succumbed to his old ways. And, God help me, I couldn't help but compare Larry's last few years to Saddam's seemingly seamless adaptation to an almost ascetic existence, washing one of his two pieces of clothing each day, praying and reading day in and day out, enjoying his small pleasures—the cigars, the "gardening," the bird-feeding. I doubt that my brother could have adapted so well. After observing the other detainees at Camp Cropper, it's clear that few had adapted so well.

My ruminations kept getting interrupted by someone announcing different numbers to get us on the right bus to get wherever we were going. In my case, it was the airport.

When my number was called I got myself into the bus, and at the airport I was pleasantly surprised to find an American there to help maneuver the airport and point out the various checkpoints. No such person had been there when I went home for my mother's funeral. This was a relief.

Finally, on the airplane I was able to relax and to sleep. It would be a long flight, with a stopover in Amsterdam. As I dozed off, I was almost jolted by my recollection of my leave-taking from Saddam. I went to see him before leaving with True Story, because I knew they were planning to move him to new quarters, possibly before I returned. I didn't want him to think I'd deserted him. So I made an unscheduled stop at his cell to tell him that I was leaving for America in one hour, and why. He understood immediately. What came next couldn't have been more of a surprise.

Saddam Hussein stood up, embraced me, and said he would be my brother.

13 | THE LAST SUPPER

LARRY WAS ONE OF THOSE PEOPLE WHO FOUND JESUS MORE THAN once, and I can only hope that his timing was right this time around. The first time was in prison many years ago and the final time was in the nursing home, where he spent his last months. He got baptized and said he had turned his life around. I don't know what accounted for the change, but I can only speculate that he'd done some serious reflecting, saw how much time he'd wasted and where it had led him, and maybe wanted to leave with a clear conscience.

All I can tell you is that I swear as he lay in his coffin there was a smile on his face. I noted that to my sister Dorothy, who agreed. We didn't talk much about it, but we both figured he had pretty much come full circle. She said only, "Mama came back to get Larry."

Mama and Larry had both been in failing health for a while, and before I got deployed I was taking him to visit Mama on Sundays. On those days she was so happy to see her two sons together. It felt like we were a family again. I would pick him up in the morning, just before lunch, and we would stay with her until it was time to take him back to the nursing home.

I didn't cut this leave short as I did after Mama's funeral. For some reason this time was different. I wanted to spend time with Rita and with my sisters and other family members. Beverly came from Las Vegas. My nieces came from Chicago and Louisville, Kentucky. My time with them seemed precious, and I wanted to make the most of it. It seemed it took a death to bring us all together.

I returned to Baghdad on August 23 through Kuwait as usual, just in time for another sandstorm. This time there was a strange orange hue to the sky that I hadn't seen before. I guess it was all that sand and dust blocking out the sun and turning the sky a strange color.

Unlike my first trip, this time I was flying, for which I was glad. No more convoys for this trip. It was hot. It always seemed the heat was more intense in Kuwait than in Iraq. It was all feeling familiar to me, but not a good kind of familiarity. I still had time on the books, and I felt I was gritting my teeth to get through it. Duty still called, and this must simply be endured.

As I anticipated, they had already moved Saddam to his new quarters while I was away, and now my time with him would be limited. Others would be in charge of his immediate care. I and a few others had already checked out his new site, partly because Sergeant Major Adams was in charge of hiring the contractors to retrofit a room in Uday's Palace for the final detention place for Saddam.

From my journal after that visit:

I visited my buddy's new home. Reality will definitely come into play now. This place looks just like what it is—a jail. A concrete slab for a bed, stainless steel sink and toilet within the cell, no garden, a small rec area, bars on the door and no sunlight. You can't see the sky by day or night.

Although he was blindfolded as usual when he was moved, I'm sure he knew that he was now living in a makeshift cell pretty much in the middle of his son's former palace. Sometime during the initial invasion, Allies had hit it with a laser-guided bomb, damaging the

Uday's Palace became Saddam's new home after $1 million was spent rehabbing it. This picture shows the palace with the roof caved in after receiving a direct hit, which it sustained quite well.

roof, the stairwell, and making a crack in the wall. No one had repaired the damage.

I think they built those places to withstand such a bombing, and it appeared to have survived well. Still, I was told that our government spent $1 million just on Saddam's new home. Just on that cell. I think somebody got bilked. If people in this country knew how much money the military spent over there, I think they'd be up at arms. Or should be.

A little to my surprise, I realized how anxious I was to see the man I was still referring to as "my buddy" or "Vic" in my journal. We were still keeping up the pretense of keeping his identity a secret, although by now most of the world knew Saddam Hussein's whereabouts. I also realized that because I'd written it so much in my diaries I was starting to think of Saddam as "Victor." I never called him that to his face. There seemed to be some irony in the name that I rather liked.

So, about 3 p.m., on my first day back, after I finished sick call at Camp Cropper but before I finished unpacking, I set off with True Story to visit Vic. It was a five- or six-mile drive from Camp Cropper, and we had to go through one checkpoint, then several layers of security once we got to the palace. Sergeant Major Carpenter visited with the officer in charge of the facility, called Project 114 in Army parlance, while I went through the various security checks to get to Saddam's quarters.

"They steal you away," he said to me, when I finally got to his cell. But he smiled broadly, gave me a hug, and asked about my family. I assured him everybody was doing fine and that it had been good to see my new wife. I told him how happy I'd been to spend time with my family, despite the sad cause of our reunion.

Despite his upbeat pretensions, I sensed he was not in top form. For sure, he was more subdued and deeper in thought, and it appeared to me that he saw the end coming. He asked about Cropper Doc and George, both of whom had rotated out by now. I took his blood pressure. It was 180 over 70, extremely high for him. We'd been keeping it quite low when he was in our care.

Then he vented for a while about his new quarters, which clearly did not pass muster. He asked why they had raised the floor and also if anyone had been swimming in the pool. I think he just wanted us to know that he knew where he was.

He also complained about the blindfold that was used every time he was moved, even to go out to the tiny rec area, which wasn't even outside. (True Story told me they had provided a treadmill for him, but he wouldn't use it.) Saddam said he knew where he was and could direct his escorts anywhere they needed to go either within the palace or without. And why, he asked, did they feel it necessary to use a helicopter to take him to his new quarters? "It's faster to drive," he said.

Old Vic might have suspected his game was almost up. I knew the doctor and medic at the new facility were having trouble keeping his blood pressure down, because Colonel Sylvester reported that they had called to ask what we had done. I asked about his medication, and sure enough, somebody had been screwing around with it. Once they put him back on the dosages we had been using, I assume things got better, because we didn't get any more calls.

A few days later on another visit, we were quite alone, and he was more introspective. We talked; he read from his poetry. He continued for a while, sitting in his chair to read something—I don't know what—and I could tell he'd been brooding about something. He asked me, "How is Iraq?"

I told him, "Not good."

I told him there was chaos: rioting, killing, kidnappings, and violence. Women feared being raped; children feared being taken away. It was bad and no one was being punished, as far as we could tell.

"They'll wish they had me back," he said.

People in the know told me there had never been such lawlessness under Saddam. I'm not sure they are right, but I suspect it was more discreet and insidious, and people who tried to buck the system just quietly disappeared. Still, since returning home, I have read how, before we invaded, Sunnis, Shia, and Christians lived in the same neighborhood and seemingly got along. Granted Saddam ruled with an iron fist, but people also knew Saddam didn't play. He would lock up anybody, including his own son. He would do away with his best friend if he considered him a dissenter. Not what you would call a nice guy, I realize.

He wanted to discuss the political situation. Why, he asked, had we invaded? Well, what he said was, "Why soldiers come?" Then, imitating them, he made a gesture like he was shooting a machine gun. He continued: "The laws here are fair. They didn't find anything," he said, referring to weapons of mass destruction. He truly had a puzzled look on his face. I told him that it was politics. Soldiers don't get caught up in politics. At least we're not supposed to. We just do the job we're sent to do.

Still, he persisted: What did America stand to gain from this? I wasn't gonna attempt to answer. I wasn't about to get into that.

During this conversation, he expressed his admiration for the late President Ronald Reagan. When Reagan was president, relations between Iraq and America were . . . and he made a long gliding motion with his hand that I took to mean "smooth." I nodded in understanding, thinking that's when some of his worst atrocities were being ignored by the Reagan administration as we—and others including Britain and France—were giving him all sorts of aid in developing nuclear, chemical, and biological weapons programs as he fought his ill-conceived war with Iran. That was when he was our guy in the Middle East, helping us by keeping Iran at bay. And it was some of the same top officials who oversaw—or perhaps winked at—the export of equipment for making weapons of mass destruction who, more than a decade later, used WMD as an excuse for invading this country and toppling its dictator.

I buttoned my lips.

After a while he perked up a bit. We started talking, and he read from his poetry. He was still writing prolifically, and, as usual, he tried to explain and interpret, both in gestures and in broken English. But I sensed a change in his attitude; he seemed to be deeper in thought these days, and his personal picture must have seemed darker.

I'm sure that his dealings with the Iraqi Tribunal was sobering. He was probably reading the tea leaves daily.

✳   ✳   ✳

WE—SADDAM AND I—DID HAVE A LAST SUPPER, ONLY WE DIDN'T know it at the time. One night, several of us managed to get away and drive up to Camp Victory North, a trip of five or six miles, because we knew the food there was better than anywhere else.

Leaving the dining facility and heading back to Cropper, we were about to pass Uday's Palace, and I decided I wanted to see Saddam. It had been a few weeks since I had visited him, but I was still on the access roster, meaning I'd been scrutinized, investigated, and cleared. I'd been on that roster since day one, so I figured I could get in.

True Story was driving and accompanied me to the building. He stayed in the front, and I went back to see Saddam. He was eating his dinner but stopped when I arrived. He asked how I was, I asked the same question, and we shook hands. He seemed glad to see me and asked me to sit down, then he took an extra plate that he had apparently saved from another meal and wiped it with one of his wet wipes. Next, he took half the meal he was eating and put it on the plate. We sat and ate together with very little conversation.

He had few complaints, except about his lack of privacy. He wondered if he could have a curtain, so that people couldn't be watching him when he used the toilet. As always, I told him I'd see what I could do. As it turned out, this time I couldn't do anything. This was out of my control; it would have been up to the Iraqis, and they weren't about to do anything to make his life easier. I mentioned earlier how they had already complained to us that what we provided was much, much too good.

Pretty soon the guards were running me off; some high-level officials were coming through, and they didn't want anybody to be seen in Saddam's cell with him. Saddam, meanwhile, had finished eating, had put down his plate, and had turned around to use his sink. Those jailhouse sinks have push-button faucets so you could only wash one hand at a time.

I walked up and touched him on the shoulder and said, "Saddam, they're running me off. I'll see you later." I told him to take care of himself, and he told me to take care of myself. By that time he was washing his mouth out with water and could only nod as he finished washing his hands. The guards were getting impatient and we didn't get to shake hands.

Once I was back in the common area, the officer in charge was at the ready, at his computer. "Okay, what did you guys talk about?" he asked. I told him, "I didn't get a chance to talk about much; you guys ran me off." I did pass on the request for a curtain across the front of Saddam's cell.

This was the last time I saw Saddam Hussein. He was washing his hands.

14 | CHECKPOINT 12

STANDING IN THE DOORWAY TO MY ROOM I COULD SEE THE RED glare from the rockets and bombs dropped by U.S. forces in what was then the most recent fight for Fallujah. Helicopters were flying back and forth; I could only assume it was pretty bad, judging by the smoke visible fifty miles to our north. Still, for some perverse reason, part of me wanted to be there, to be in on the action, to see for myself what was going on.

Fallujah was important, but at the time I didn't know exactly how important. Part of its importance was strategic: it is on the main road to Baghdad. Part of its importance was historical: it has been inhabited since Babylonian times. Most recently, it has been influential under Iraqi independence and the oil wealth. The military considered it important because so many Sunni Muslims and Ba'ath Party officials loyal to Saddam Hussein lived there. The insurgency, in other words.

Heavily industrialized, the city had several large factories, one of which was suspected of being used for making chemical weapons. That factory was closed years ago—in the 1990s—by the United Nations Special Commission (UNSCOM). Although the city fared well after the invasion and the Iraqi Army appeared to abandon its position, there was heavy looting, especially of former government sites.

Fallujah was also near the now-infamous Abu Ghraib prison, from which Saddam—shortly before he was deposed and for reasons known only to him—had ordered the prisoners released. I guess he just wanted to make things as difficult as possible for the invaders. In addition to the Iraqi Army, we had "Ali Baba" to deal with— thugs and thieves and murderers at large. ("Ali Baba" is a term I picked up from an older Iraqi woman named Sahira, who worked as a housekeeper at a place where the Army sent us for R and R.)

The insurgency at Fallujah was strong and had on several occasions defied American curfews. This is also the place where four American contractors were dragged from their cars, beaten, and set on fire. A picture of their burned corpses hanging from a bridge over the Euphrates is an image that most Americans won't forget and was one of the most incendiary events of the war. The men— contractors from Blackwater USA—were in a convoy when it was ambushed, and the bridge is probably known as "Blackwater Bridge" to this day. It certainly was when I was there.

We probably would not have known about the incident at the time, but thanks to the Internet—our link to the outside world—we were able to see pictures of those charred bodies dangling from the bridge at the same time that America did. By then, I was almost numb when it came to death and destruction, but this really pissed me off. It was so unnecessary.

Later, I learned that almost one hundred American Marines were killed and more than one thousand wounded in this Fallujah battle that I was watching from the safety of Camp Cropper. After our military eventually recaptured the city in an operation known as Phantom Fury, our forces discovered beheading chambers and bomb-making factories, both of which were touted as evidence of Fallujah's role in the insurgency.

After the battle, my path crossed briefly with that of a captain

Housing outside of Camp Cropper. Too close for comfort, in my book.

from the 112th MP Battalion from Canton, Mississippi, who was there in Fallujah. I remembered him from his short stay at Cropper months before. He told me about how the Americans had tried to evacuate the women and children before the fighting started. Boys over fifteen were detained, however. But whaddaya know, the women didn't want to leave their husbands and sons, so they managed to return to the city in full knowledge that the battle was about to begin.

They faced near-certain death with their family members. It has haunted me, and I had to ask myself—why would I have wanted to be there? I later saw figures that showed that more than 1,350 insurgent fighters were killed in that operation. I always wondered how many women and children were included in that figure.

Meanwhile, we were having our own problems with the insurgency. For the most part, we felt that Camp Cropper was the safest place to be, because so much of the insurgency was made up of people loyal to Saddam and his regime. Therefore, the reasoning went, they would want to keep him safe. But that didn't make us totally invulnerable. Sometimes the hatred for Americans overcame their love of the regime leaders. Maybe some had thoughts of actually springing their former leaders. We had our share of mortar attacks and if the launch was close enough, you could actually hear it. Once, a mortar round landed inside the camp. The detainees were outside for recreation when this happened, and it was almost comical the way they scattered to their rooms. Luckily, no one was hurt.

One major safety issue was our proximity to the airport, which came in handy in many instances, but it was a negative on the security scale. The airport was an obvious target: it was well-lit, there was a control tower that could be seen from many observation points, and there were always plenty of soldiers there. It became a favorite target.

This is the C141 we rode to Kuwait.

Sometimes the many mortar rounds and rockets aimed at the airport fell short and we'd have to take cover.

One time, Delta Company, which provided all our MP escorts, was having a formation right outside the sallyport and a mortar round hit there, injuring several of their soldiers. We treated them initially at Camp Cropper, then took them to the 118th for further treatment. Most of the injuries were from shrapnel. About twenty minutes earlier there had been a much larger formation, and it would have been a whole lot worse.

Unfortunately, our feeling of relative security was confined to the times we were actually in Camp Cropper. Because there were so few of us in the 439th, we had to take turns going to meet Iraqi contractors and their workers for projects inside the camp. Adams set it all up, and we dealt regularly with a guy named Ali, who could negotiate the number of workers and the time he would need for a specific job.

They met us regularly at Checkpoint 4 a few miles west of Camp Cropper, and I don't mind admitting that this place always made me nervous. It must have made others nervous too because the status here was always red—we were always notified by our commanders about the status before we started anywhere—which meant you were locked and loaded: you locked in your magazine, loaded a round in the chamber, and took your selector switch off "safe." In other words, you're ready to fire. I always carried an M-16 and a 9 mm handgun; if anything happened, I wasn't going out by myself. I would take a few with me. Soldiers were stationed on the rooftops of surrounding buildings, ready to fire if anything happened. Still, it was scary.

This was an enclosed staging area, necessitating going out into a sea of people to find the contractors we wanted. A rocket or mortar round could be dropped in here, and it would all be over. A suicide bomber could easily be in this mix as well. I was suspicious of everybody, even though I know most are just looking for a job. They

Two contractors working on a gymnasium at Camp Cropper.

had ID cards that were highly suspect, but for some crazy reason these cards were accepted. Some had no photo ID, others used IDs that were pictures of small children, supposedly the ID holder as a child. But who could tell? And who would argue?

After I got my contractor and workers, I loaded them on a bus and headed back to camp. I knew I wasn't the only one running a risk here; the contractors and workers were targeted by the bad guys for working with the Americans. They were often shot at and also received death threats. They had to quit work at 4:30 p.m. on the dot, so they could be in their houses before it got dark at 5 p.m. It was a very rigid, self-imposed curfew that started at darkness. No matter what, they had to leave at the appointed hour.

Once, Ali's nephew was kidnapped and held for ransom. His life was spared, but after the money was paid, he promptly left Iraq. Apparently, he had been targeted because Ali was working with the Americans.

Back at the camp, Ali and the workers he had chosen did innumerable tasks for us, including construction projects such as installing new toilets and washbasins. They built a gymnasium for all the soldiers at Camp Cropper and also renovated what we called the 439th building, including a courtroom that in the end wasn't used much. I'm pretty sure that it was used only for the arraignments of Saddam and the other eleven henchmen. I can always identify that room in pictures, because Adams specified that it be painted in yellow and green, the colors of the 439th. I have to give Ali and his boys credit; they did a good job.

Although I spent most of my time in the clinic, the thought of Iraqis working inside our camp was always a little unsettling. We had no way of telling if any of them were sympathetic to the insurgency. Whenever I saw them looking around, I wondered if they were actually sizing up the camp. My anxiety level was especially high those days. Even with guards standing alongside the workers, it's hard to watch a person work and watch your surroundings too.

Another reason for my high anxiety was that it seemed I was making a trip to the CSH almost every other day. Not only did we have to take detainees there, but we also took lab work for analysis. Then we had to go back and get the results. I tried to get them to e-mail me the results, but that never happened.

More and more frequently, it was falling to me to make these dangerous trips because of an unfortunate incident in which one of the medics who ordinarily would have taken a share of the trips was badly injured and sent home. Although no one was killed, everyone in his vehicle was hurt, some worse than others. The four of them were on their way back to the 118th after making a trip to the Green Zone in downtown Baghdad. All I know is that they did not have an MP escort, and I suspect it was some sort of egomania and/or arrogance that caused an otherwise good officer to make the trip with two en-listed men and another officer of lesser rank, without the MP escort. The escort was not mandatory, but it was foolhardy, to say the least.

One of the guys who regularly accompanied the ranking officer told me they were always fearful because they never had the MP escort, which would have had .50-caliber machine guns that commanded a lot of respect. We, the medical people, could only carry M-16s, which wouldn't have helped a lot in this particular case. They ran into a suicide bomber after they left the Green Zone. The insurgents look for soft targets, and they fit the profile.

Although I wasn't with them, I was nevertheless affected. After an investigation, members of the 118th were forbidden to go outside the coalition-controlled areas, meaning my life suddenly became even more complicated. And I was really pissed off. With the medics from the 118th out of the rotation, I found I was traveling much more than usual. I mention this incident only to explain why my anxiety level was higher than usual these days.

On one hot, dry, dusty day in early October, we had traveled the dreaded Route Irish to take detainee No. 36 to the CSH for anemia and heart palpitations.

A word about Route Irish. I think each time I discuss it, I precede it with the word *dreaded*. About seven miles long, it connected downtown Baghdad with the airport, and it was about the only straight shot between the two. Route Tampa, which I discussed in an earlier chapter, is the other route we sometimes used; Tampa goes through Sadr City, also not a pleasant prospect.

I read that Route Irish averaged one attack per day, and every time I traveled it, I knew it was a crapshoot. The charred remnants of vehicles along the way tell the story better than I can. It's very hard to check for roadside bombs when you're traveling at sixty miles an hour. Plus, they can be hidden in the guardrails, burlap sacks, and even in animal carcasses, which were not uncommon along the road. VIPs and other higher ups knew it was too dangerous to travel; they took helicopters from the Green Zone to the APOD. I have since read that some security firm was getting more than three thousand dollars for a one-way trip in a bullet-proof taxi.

Tank outside the walls of Camp Cropper.

You might wonder if we were compromising our charges' safety (to say nothing of our own) for non-life-threatening matters, but we felt we couldn't take chances, especially with heart issues or chest pains. Some were real, most were not. But the Abu Ghraib cloud was hanging low.

On this particular mission, I was in the fourth vehicle of a convoy, the detainee was riding in the Humvee in front, and two others were providing the standard military-police escort. All four were equipped with .50-caliber machine guns. Now we were in the Green Zone, the heavily fortified area in downtown Baghdad where the government and diplomatic buildings are located. It's supposedly safe, but really it's just heavily fortified.

We had just cleared Checkpoint 12, the only checkpoint for this particular trip.

As always, the detainee was blindfolded. Our method of "blindfolding" was to use goggles with the lenses and sides covered with tape. They couldn't see a thing, and it seemed more humane than putting hoods over their heads. He was shackled and handcuffed and wore a helmet and body armor along with the rest of us. We'd had lots of eye injuries from the flying shrapnel, so goggles were mandatory for American soldiers entering the Green Zone. Goggles were among the items they checked for at the checkpoints.

I heard an explosion, and I looked to my left and saw a big, black cloud of smoke coming from a car that had just blown up. It seemed the bombers were targeting the Humvee I was in because they let everyone else go through. Why, I don't know. But thanks to a conveniently placed concrete barrier, we were unharmed. I will never know if the car-bomb planners expected the explosives to take out the blast wall as well, or if they were just trying to create mayhem. They certainly did that.

Anyway, the blast wall took the brunt of the explosion. I don't like thinking about what would have happened if it hadn't been where it was. This time we were in an armored vehicle, but I'm not sure that would have helped us.

This was just one of several explosions in the area, and others were not so fortunate. Apparently, a hotel where some American contractors and journalists were staying also was targeted. By this time, we were in downtown Baghdad, and right at the back entrance to the CSH. We got there just ahead of the casualties. Here, we could maybe do some good. The situation was what we call "mascal," a military term meaning more casualties than the capacity to care for them.

The emergency room was quickly filled, and once I slipped and almost went sprawling because of the slick floor—slick because of all the blood. We were treating people everywhere—in the halls and waiting rooms, the eye clinic, and in any other nook and cranny we could find. The injured included Iraqi civilians and American contractors.

This is fucked up! I wanted to scream. *This should not be happening.* My buddy Matt was interpreting, and I was dressing wounds. All I could say was the F-word. All of these innocent people were caught up in this madness. I thought I might start having palpitations myself. Matt and I helped out as long as we could. Someone had found the time to check our detainee, who had a bleeding ulcer it turned out. That we can handle, with medication that we received at the CSH.

It was starting to get dark, and we had to return to camp, which meant running another gauntlet through the snipers and bombers, wondering if we would be next. The more trips I made to the CSH, the more I felt I was rolling the dice, and sooner or later I'd roll snake eyes. I tried not to think about it, but sometimes it was hard not to. I was also struck by the fact that all this craziness was taking place during Ramadan, when everything should have been peaceful.

The *Stars and Stripes,* a newspaper for the soldiers, carried an account of this particular incident, one of several that were carried out within an hour of each other, killing at least twenty-one people and wounding ninety-six. They were representative of a growing campaign of car bombings the insurgency was conducting. The previous month had seen thirty-nine such bombings, the highest incidence since our invasion.

Within the next two months, I got caught up in at least two more such incidents while transporting our detainees for medical attention.

"Here we go again," I said to myself when casualties from Balad came in by helicopter one day when I had made another trek to the CSH. Balad is about sixty-eight kilometers north of Baghdad, in the Sunni Triangle. Again, Matt and I helped, but I was starting to get weary. The Iraqi National Guard was the group that took the hit that day.

Probably the worst of all was on November 7. "*Mascal at the CSH,*" my journal reads. I had brought No. 165 for a CT scan of his head after he had complained of severe headaches and vision problems. I don't know how they found time to do the scan because very soon the place was hoppin'.

Elite British forces—the Black Watch Group, to be specific—were coming in by vehicle and by helicopter. I only know who they were because I saw their uniforms. There was no time for formalities, such as introductions. I was not a formal part of this effort, but I couldn't help but do a personal triage of these casualties, meaning I was deciding the categories of care that would be needed: immediate, minimal, delayed, and expectant. The latter, I'm sorry to say, means that person is going to die and we need to use our precious time to save lives we know can be saved. "Conserve the fighting strength," is the operative maxim.

The casualties I was facing included a bilateral amputee, traumatic right leg amputee, several with severe shrapnel facial wounds, multiple burns, and a DOA for which we needed a body bag. Many were unconscious and very quiet—so quiet that I wondered if they had been given morphine by combat medics even before they got here.

Oh, this was ugly. I work in surgery for a living, but seeing my comrades-in-arms coming in like this, I thought I was going to be sick. I've seen amputations, gunshot wounds, people with burns on 90 percent of their bodies, but this is different. I guess it's more on a personal level. These are people I might have been standing shoulder to shoulder with. These are my brothers. This is the sort of thing that will haunt me for years to come.

As far as the triage went, I didn't see anyone who would fit in the "minimal" category. These people were in bad shape. I managed to pull myself together and hang tough. Unfortunately, Rumsfeld's callous words a month later would have a certain validity: Some of these guys *were* riding in Bradleys, troop carriers that are, indeed, armored. It must have been one hell of an explosion.

My head hurt, and my stomach was knotted. My selfish thoughts were that I was getting too short to keep making these trips to the CSH. Getting "short" is a military expression meaning that your time is just about up, that you're getting close to the end of your tour of duty. When you get to one hundred days before your tour of duty is up, you start counting down. Then you're a "double-digit midget," and that's a very good thing. When you get down to being a single-digit midget, you're so short you can't step up on the curb. It's a good feeling.

At this point, I was a double-digit midget. My own countdown had started.

15 | GOING HOME

I*T'S CHRISTMAS EVE AND I'M STILL MAKING TRIPS TO THE CSH. TODAY IT was to get a CT of the abdomen for numbers 84 and 90. We needed to rule out pancreatic cancer for #90 and cholecystitis for #84.*

I suspected they were both making up their symptoms. We left them at the hospital for evaluation.

Christmas dawned cloudy and rainy. We were back in the rainy season, much like when we arrived a little less than a year ago. I remembered the previous Christmas back in St. Louis on my prized three-day pass.

Sick call was suspended, meaning the clinic wasn't open for Christmas, and, fortunately, there were no incidents to occupy us. I didn't write much in my journal except for:

Sitting in my room listening to Charlie Brown Xmas CD.
(There are some good jazzy tunes on that CD, by the way.)

Next day I wrote:

#165 refused breakfast. On hunger strike?

I always had more than passing interest in this guy. I'd met him about a month earlier in the clinic as he was being checked in, and he was not in good condition. He had been worked over pretty good by somebody before he came to us, and he claimed not to know who did it. Both his eyes were really red—blood red, beyond bloodshot. He had lots of bruises around his kidneys and multiple abrasions and bruises on his legs. He said he'd blacked out during the beating. I believed his claim that he did not know his assailant, or assailants. I suspect they didn't reveal their identity. But I have my own idea about who did it, and let's just leave it at that.

Obviously, I had to watch him carefully to change his leg dressings and to make sure the wounds were healing properly. He spoke good English, and somewhere along the way I learned he had two wives, one who lived in Iowa with their ten-year-old son. She was pregnant. His second wife lived in Jordan.

When he told me about his wife and son back in the States, I couldn't help but ask, "What are you doing over here?" He never said another word. I could only conclude he'd come for jihad. And got caught.

On the day after Christmas—about midnight on a Sunday—I received a call on my radio. It was from higher headquarters to the effect that I needed to take this guy to the CSH to be checked out with a full-body CT scan.

"Fuck," I believe I said. "It's midnight." But I got myself dressed, got my weapons, put on my body armor, and went to the TOC (technical operations center) where I met my MP escort from Delta Company. No. 165 was there and ready to go. The trip to the CSH was uneventful. He was checked out and found not to have any life-threatening injuries. But I also saw why the general wanted him checked out. His injuries could have been more extensive than those we could see. We especially feared internal bleeding.

But I had other things to fret about these days, and they had nothing to do with injured detainees and how they got that way.

My worries didn't have much to do with the goings-on at Camp Cropper. They had everything to do with how much I wanted to get out of there. I wrote:

> *The 31st CSH is rotating out soon, and will be replaced by the 86th CSH from Fort Campbell, Ky. Everybody is leaving except us. Why are we still here?*

It was getting more dangerous here by the minute. The cavalry was doing ID checks in full battle rattle because of an unfortunate incident at another camp. An Iraqi contractor who had been working at the camp for two or three months turned out to be a suicide bomber. He had been a good worker, friendly, and gained the trust of the soldiers, who apparently let their guard down. It may have been the first and only time he wasn't frisked, but it was the last. He took twenty-two people with him in a mess hall at lunchtime at the U.S. base near Mosul, slightly more than two hundred miles away.

I felt slightly vindicated in being so distrustful of the Iraqi workers. They performed so many jobs at the bases—cooking, construction, and even office work—but I always felt distracted by them, feeling I needed to watch them, watch my back, and do my job at the same time. Now, I would no longer feel any guilt for my suspicion.

The work went on, in spite of the many distractions, including preparations for getting out of Iraq. On December 29, we went back to the CSH to get Nos. 90 and 84, and the next day, we took No. 87 for abdominal pains.

The biggest news of New Year's Eve Day, 2004: Ramsey Clark came to join Saddam's legal team. Adams told me, casually, that Clark had arrived. I was incredulous. "*The* Ramsey Clark, the former U.S. attorney general?"

"That's the one," Adams said.

Colonel Sylvester surprised us on New Year's Eve with some Cuban cigars that Vic's family had sent him. He couldn't have them at the new quarters—remember he was not under U.S. control any longer, and I'm sure they would have disapproved of any such pleasantries. So we—we happy few in the 439th—sat outside on a relatively pleasant evening and smoked. And we contemplated our imminent departure.

Now Christmas and New Year's had come and gone and still no sign of our replacements. To say I was ready to leave this place was an understatement, but to invoke a military cliché, death before dishonor and all that good stuff.

We knew it couldn't be too long. We had partially cleared customs two weeks before. That was for our footlockers and other equipment. For that, the Army sent a special unit to set up a "sterile" area where they inspected everything we had in our footlockers. We took out everything, they inspected it, and then re-packed our footlockers, put the lock back on it, and put it inside a big metal container called a conex. The conex usually leaves thirty days before you do, and you don't see your stuff until you get back to your mobilization site.

Going through customs. Now you know you're going home.

I thought they would never get here, but our replacements finally arrived on January 4, and for the next few days we did left seat/ right seat training, which is a technical term for job shadowing. Meanwhile, of course, time did not stand still. No. 25 fell and hurt his right hip, and—guess what—this time I had one of the medics from the 118th take him to the APOD, where the Air Force docs would X-ray his hip and pelvis. Back in the fall, trying to limit our trips to the CSH, I'd finally wised up to the fact that maybe some of these very dangerous trips could be avoided if certain minor procedures could be done closer to "home." The Air Force doc I proposed this to was receptive to the idea. Were it not for his help, I would have been going to the CSH even more than I did.

Meanwhile, the 439th was headed to North Victory for outgoing briefings. I noticed that several of the windows in our briefing building were boarded up, a result of a mortar attack the night before. We returned back to Cropper in near-delirious anticipation of our departure. True Story and I were riding together and noted the darkness on this cloudy night. I'd say that our mood was a combination of jubilation and trepidation of some unforeseen last-minute snafu. Tomorrow, we would pack and head for the APOD, this time for good.

We spent our last night in our room playing spades and laughing about all the games I won playing with Vic, whose butt I used to spank regularly. That's a joke that maybe only Ron Adams and I would get: each night when I'd start out for my evening rounds to the wood, Adams would say, "Don't be down there playing spades." And I'd say, "Yeah, and I spank his butt regularly."

From my journal:

1/13/05 0600 wakeup, 0830 load up and head for the APOD. I should be getting excited. It's been a long time since something moved me. Although I'm glad to be leaving, there still seems to be an emotional void inside. I guess I've suppressed my feelings for too long.

At the APOD, we loaded all our bags onto an Air Force pallet, secured them with web-like cargo straps, and then watched television in a waiting room until we saw our plane—a C-130—rolling down the strip. We departed the APOD at 2 p.m. and arrived at Camp Doha in Kuwait at 4 p.m.

Chillin' in Kuwait, I wrote in my journal. *It seems kind of strange to be walking around without a weapon and body armor. I still can't keep myself from looking all around, my head on a swivel at all times, constantly on the watch for a place to take cover.*

I clearly wasn't adjusted to being out of the combat zone. On the other hand, it had only been a couple of hours.

We found our sleeping area, and I got my cot and put away my gear. There was a clean, well-lit place to shower, and in the bright white-walled shower the water seemed especially clean. For sure it stayed hot longer than we were used to.

Kuwait is a progressive Muslim country, and wealthy too. I went to the PX and bought two cigars to smoke: one for the completed mission and one for a safe trip home. Still no time to reflect.

I ran into Dr. Robert Wilkins; he was living in a building across from us. He had been the last doc on my tour, and we had spent a lot of time together. We smoked a cigar together and took a stroll around the camp. After two days in Kuwait, it was time for the next leg: to Frankfurt.

But first we had to clear customs, which involved dumping the entire contents of our bags and pockets for inspection. There was also an amnesty station set up where we could deposit items that we shouldn't have had with no questions asked. The amnesty is your last chance to save yourself before they wand you and scan you to make sure you're not taking anything classified or illegal back to the States. If soldiers still had those grenades, they could have dumped them here, rather than in our Porta Johns. But once you get to the scanning area, all bets are off. Now, if you are caught with something you're not supposed to have, you can get all kinds of grief, including a big delay or even a court martial.

We then boarded the plane en route to Germany, where we landed in Bonn instead of Frankfurt. I can't remember the reason for the change of course. It must not have been anything serious, because we didn't even deplane.

I was losing track of the days, but at some point I determined that it was January 16. After a couple hours in Bonn, we were off to Shannon, Ireland, for refueling. We were allowed two hours here to go to the duty free shop in the airport. There, I ran into Doc Wilkins again. At Shannon, I bought two shot glasses for my collection. I have them from every country I've visited, finding them an easy thing to collect because of their size. At this writing, I probably have a collection of maybe fourteen glasses.

Meanwhile, some American tourists bought us, along with some 10th Mountain Division soldiers, a beer and posed for pictures with us and *thanked* us for our service to our country. It made me feel good. It made me feel proud to be an American. It felt good to feel good again.

That beer tasted oh so good. It was the first drink of alcohol that we had had in a long time. Then we had a second. Those beers, coupled with some Flexeril I had in my pocket for many willing takers, assured a nice sleep as we crossed the Big Pond for what I hoped would be the last time for a while.

Next stop was Fort Drum in upper New York State, where we let off the soldiers from the other division. Back in the U.S. of A. we were, and it was about 10 p.m., cold and windy on this January night. But I didn't care. I walked down the steps from the plane and laid down right there, spread eagled on the cold tarmac. Thank you, Jesus. I was so glad to be back. Then, we went to Fort Riley, Kansas, and, lastly, to Fort Omaha, Nebraska, to turn in all our equipment. Eleven days after leaving Baghdad, I was back home in St. Louis.

The next month I headed out again, this time for a seven-day cruise with Rita, in the western Caribbean. This was our honeymoon.

I bought some Cuban cigars in the Grand Cayman Islands and then, a tropical drink in hand, dressed only in my robe and house shoes, I watched the sunset one night from my balcony on the cruise ship called *The Victory*. As I smoked one of the cigars, I thought of the man who taught me how. In fact, I said, "This one's for Vic."

Somehow I can't get this man out of my mind, and I fear I may never. He's being compared to both Joseph Stalin and Adolph Hitler, and I understand why he was so reviled. "Kill him slow," said the Kurds I knew, as they made a slow slicing motion with their hands. (Cut his throat slowly and let him suffer?)

But I also remember how much I had enjoyed Saddam's company, even when I suffered pangs of guilt in the enjoyment. I wonder what that says about me. Maybe it says that if the nurse and the soldier were in combat, the nurse would have won. I know that some people think the guy just got to me, that I let my guard down too far, that I'm naïve. I prefer to think that in being a neutral good soldier, I just recognized his humanity. And, eventually, I let myself care.

I took another sip of my drink and a drag of the cigar and thought of this man who had known every luxury imaginable, then once in prison made his own toothpicks out of small twigs he'd pick up in his dusty outdoor recreation area.

I remember how he washed his own *dishdasha* each day rather than stepping into an expensively tailored suit, how he slept on a cot— and later a concrete slab covered with a foam rubber pad—rather than on pillows covered with silk. I remember his adjustment to life in an eight-by-ten cell, after having his pick of several palaces. I remember the absolute joy on his face when I found him some honey for his pancakes one day.

"How do you adjust to living with none of your usual luxuries?" I asked him that day.

"I remember how I grew up, a simple and poor farmer," he responded. And when he made himself coffee, stirring the instant coffee into cold water with his finger, he'd just shrug and say,

"What we do, what we do." Or when the air-conditioner failed on a particularly hot day and he sat, his *dishdasha* down around his waist, and fanned himself with his notepad, again repeating, "What we do, what we do," with a calm smile.

I think maybe I knew his type, and I think my subconscious had been noodling over this all the time I was tending to him. He was once a street fighter like I was when I was a kid. I was fighting thugs and bullies in the projects; he was fighting gangs in Tikrit and later in Baghdad. He was playing for much higher stakes, and his rise to power is almost astonishing considering his beginnings. I settled for a safer, middle-class route, but I'm alive to tell it.

Now that I'm safely away from it all, I have time to think about some of the strange overlappings of our lives, but the catch is, I'm not sure I want to. But I think I may have an inkling why this man got under my skin the way he did.

I know a little about his childhood because I've done some research since returning home. Most of his biographical accounts start out something like this: "Saddam Hussein, the son of a landless peasant, was born in 1937. . . ." Many times that "landless" thing comes up.

Many accounts say he was born in Tikrit, a Sunni stronghold, but he was actually born in a small village near there, in the mud hut of his uncle. It was a village of mostly thugs and thieves. His mother, Sabha, had gone there after her husband—Saddam's father—died. Her new husband was extremely cruel and beat Saddam with a stick covered with asphalt.

And although I'm not drawing precise parallels to his early life and mine, I can't help but be struck with how we both started our lives with a shared conviction that the outside world was a mean and hostile place, that we had only our own wits and wiles to rely on, and that we had to watch our backs at all times.

He carried an iron bar to fend off attacks of other boys; I carried a knife. Among his male relatives, killing was some sort of a rite of passage, and when he was a young teenager, he killed a shepherd from a nearby tribe. He added three more murders while still in his teens.

Until now I haven't told but a handful of people, but when I was thirteen, I killed a kid too, in a long-ago episode that I have spent a good part of my life trying to forget. He was three years older, maybe thirty pounds heavier, and almost a foot taller. He was a bully. It happened one night as I waited with my friend James for his mother, who was coming home from work. I agreed when he asked me to stay with him, because I knew—indeed, everyone in our building knew—she'd been raped not long before. We all needed protection, and I carried a hunting knife I'd bought at a sporting goods store.

As we sat and waited on a warm April night, this bully and his buddy started hassling and threatening us, then hauled off and hit me in the chest, nearly knocking me off the bench. He hit me a second time and then I pulled out my knife and said, "Don't hit me no more." He said something to the effect that if I ever pulled a knife on him again, I'd better kill him. At that point, we turned to go to my apartment and he followed us to my door. Suddenly, he was on me, and I raised my hand and struck out, knife in hand. I don't remember much about the fight, but I know we fought, and I fought hard. I'm sure I thought I was fighting for my life. Then I saw him stagger away and walk up the steps to the next floor. As soon as James and I got inside, we blurted out what had happened to my mother, and she called the police. The kid must have bled to death waiting for the ambulance.

I had a public defender who was nice but didn't do such a good job for me. Justifiable homicide the jury called it, and I spent almost a year in detention. I was never, ever in another fight after that, and I will say that nobody hassled me or my family again.

I'm not suggesting that this long-ago stabbing gave me much in common with Saddam Hussein, but when I consider the big picture of our early beginnings, I think maybe I had sensed a subconscious bond with a man who had undergone much more violence in his early life that I could have imagined.

Certainly, it gave me no sympathy for Saddam's documented cruelty to both people and animals. I read somewhere that he would bring his iron bar to a red heat then stab an animal in the stomach. I tried to make that image jibe with my favorite image of Saddam with the birds flocking around when he went outside to water the small, dusty plot where he was trying to grow a garden. I wondered why he would bother to save his limited rations to feed some birds when he tortured and killed so many human beings. I'm not sure I'll ever reconcile Saddam's cruel side with this kindly man I watched feed the birds. But I think I saw him come to grips with his past. I know he'd convinced himself that everything he did was for Iraq, and now, especially after talking to George, I think he accepted both his imprisonment without fear and his execution as not only inevitable but a way to ensure his legacy.

Reluctantly, I admire that. If nothing else—for better or for worse—he had faith in himself.

It was a tough time for me, that tour in Iraq. As I tried to stay focused on the mission, I think I hardened. I was ready to kill on a moment's notice, and for reasons I think you can understand, that scares me. Mostly, I think I hardened because I had to put my feelings aside so many times that now I'm having trouble letting them come back.

To this day, the void is still there, but maybe not as large as it was, and I'm aware of it less frequently. I would like to think that eventually I could fill my own inner emptiness with an increased spirituality. I have always envisioned going back to Iraq, and I may yet, if and when things settle down, which won't be any time soon. I wonder if that would be cathartic; maybe just seeing the country and the people we felt we were so ineffectively fighting for could be helpful.

Funny, I'd never given much thought to what's inside my heart and soul before the Iraq experience.

Funny, if a Quran-carrying, jihad-spouting, opportunistic, evil, and narcissistic mass murderer could make me more devout, more spiritual, and more accepting of my own final destiny. But I think he did. I hope he did.

The 439th after a job well done.

The Camp Cropper clinic crew: Joe, an interpreter, me, Susan, Doc Wilkins, and Abby.

EPILOGUE

I T WAS THE LAST FRIDAY NIGHT OF 2006, TWO DAYS BEFORE THE end of the year. A story about my relationship with Saddam Hussein was scheduled to run in the *St. Louis Post-Dispatch* the next week. The television was on, but I hadn't been watching. All of the sudden I heard the announcer saying that Saddam Hussein was about to be executed, and I made a beeline for the couch in the family room.

We all know the story about how someone smuggled the camera phone into the execution chamber, and now I was watching the final minutes of Vic or "my buddy" or No. 001 or HVD #1 or the Ace of Spades.

The picture was grainy and a little jerky, but there he was, the noose slipping over his head. He looked sober, grim really, but not scared. He was wearing the coat that Seavey and Adams got for him, and somehow that moved me, remembering the way Seavey had described how much Saddam loved the coat and how happy he'd been to give up the orange prison coat that he'd formerly been given.

I saw him refuse the hood so he could look his executioners in the eye, even as the rope tightened around his neck and the onlookers heckled him. He didn't cry or plead or beg. He was being heckled while in his shackles and handcuffs, and he seemed to smile sardonically when he said to the guards, "Is this how you show your bravery?"

He was the most dignified person there. This was a man who was not afraid to die. According to George, it was a moment that Saddam had been waiting for. But if he hoped it would secure his legacy and assure his place in history, I think he hoped in vain.

In seconds, it was over, and Saddam dropped, lifeless, through the trap door. The man I had just watched hang to death was the same man who ruled Iraq with a regime of fear, the man who was convicted of unbelievable atrocities that included murdering thousands of his own countrymen, the man they called "the butcher of Baghdad."

He was a monster, and he had been condemned to die by a court ruling, an exercise in justice he had denied so many others. This was the man for whom America had launched an invasion to topple and a man who, indirectly, had been responsible for the deaths of more than four thousand of my fellow countrymen.

* * *

I AM WARM AND SAFE IN THE COMFORT OF MY HOME HERE IN Normandy, Missouri, but I find myself shivering. I think maybe I'm shivering because my feelings are so mixed and I'm so conflicted. I want to deal with this, and I'll try, but I'm not sure how. I know I should actively hate this man who is responsible for so much evil, but it's hard to hate someone who treated me with respect and kindness, who hugged me when my brother died and who shared a meager meal with me and showed me nothing but respect.

I know I should hate him, but it's not easy.

He'd had a profound effect on me, and I'm still sorting out why. I guess I will be 'til the day I die.

SOURCES

BOOKS

Anderson, Dale. *Saddam Hussein*. Minneapolis: Lerner Publications Company, 2004, p. 61.

Reuters. *Saddam's Iraq*. New York: Prentice Hall, 2003, pp. 44–45, 48–51, 130–31.

Munthe, Turi, ed. *The Saddam Hussein Reader: Selections from Leading Writers on Iraq*. New York: Thunder's Mouth Press, 2002, pp. 3–36, 82–87, 215.

McClellan, Scott. *What Happened*. New York: Public Affairs, 2008, pp. 121, 126, 144, 160, 200.

WEBSITES

AlJazeera.net. "'Chemical Ali' Sentenced to Death," March 2, 2009.

AnnistonStar.com, Slobodan Lekic, "Mess Hall Probably Hit by Suicide Bomber, U.S. Military Says," Associated Press, December 23, 2004.

BBC News, Middle East, Paul Harris, "Inside 'Chemical Ali's' Palace," April 4, 2003.

BBC News, World Edition, "Iraq's Most Wanted," September 5, 2004.

BBC News, Middle East, "Iraq's Women Scientists, Profile: Dr. Huda Salih Madhi Ammash," September 22, 2004.

BBC News, Magdi Abdelhadi, "Witness Tells of Saddam's Last Moments," BBC Middle East Analyst, January 13, 2007.

BBC News, "Saddam Hussein's Top Aides Hanged," January 15, 2007.

BBC News, Middle East, "Profile: 'Chemical Ali,'" February 29, 2008.

CNN.com./World, "Pentagon: Iraqi Woman Dubbed 'Mrs. Anthrax' in Custody," May 5, 2003.

CNN.com, "Suicide Bomber Suspected in Mess Hall Attack," December 25, 2004.

CNN.com/World, David Ensor, "U.S. Captures Mastermind of Achille Lauro Hijacking," April 16, 2003.

CNN World News, Rob Reynolds, "Abu Abbas: From Terrorist to Peace Advocate," May 10, 1996.

Common Dreams.org, "Reagan Played Decisive Role in Saddam Hussein's Survival in Iran-Iraq War," June 9, 2004.

CounterPunch, "How Reagan Armed Saddam with Chemical Weapons," June 17, 2004.

Counterpunch, Abu Spinoza, "Dr. Huda Ammash's Detention, Jailed for Exposing Costs of Sanctions & War?" May 8, 2003.

Democracy Now! The War and Peace Report, June 9, 2004.

Frontline, KETC Channel 9, interview with Tariq Aziz, no date.

Global Policy Forum, Sabrina Tavernise, "Sectarian Hatred Pulls Apart Iraq's Mixed Towns," New York Times, November 20, 2005.

Guardian.co.uk, Peter Beaumont, Paul Harris and Antony Barnett, "Inside Secret Saddam Prison," The Observer, May 22, 2005.

The Guardian, Unlimited Special Reports, Julian Borger in Washington and Jonathan Steele, "US Gives Up Search for Saddam's WMD," January 13, 2005.

International Herald Tribune, Sabrina Tavernise, "Iraqi Shiites Seize Sunni Neighborhoods in Baghdad," December 23, 2006.

International Justice Tribunals, "Tariq Aziz Goes on Trial," by Thijs Bouwknegt, April 24, 2008.

Iran Military Forum, Iran Military.Net, "Saddam's Wives," July 29, 2007.

IslamOnline.net, "Iraqi Scientists in US Custody," Live Dialogue, May 31, 2004.

MSNBC News, Lisa Myers & the NBC investigative unit, "In Custody, Aziz Ready to Name Names," December 17, 2004.

New York Times, Stephen C. Pelletiere, "A War Crime or an Act of War?" January 31, 2003.

New York Times, Middle East, "Iraqi Leaders Say the Way Is Clear for the Execution of 'Chemical Ali'," March 1, 2008.

New York Times, Middle East, Andrew E. Kramer, "Mastermind of '80s Gas Attacks on Kurds is Taken to a Gallows Site in Baghdad," October 18, 2007.

NBC News, Robert Windrem, "Ex-Saddam Defense Minister Set to be Executed," October 12, 2007.

Seattle Post-Intelligencer, Larry Johnson, "Iraqi Cancers, Birth Defects Blamed on U.S. Depleted Uranium," November 12, 2002.

Sydney Morning Herald, Paul McGeough, "The World's Most Dangerous Road," June 8, 2005.

Trial Watch, trial-ch.org, "Barzan Ibrahim Hassan al-Tikriti," January 2007.

Yahoo!News, Singapore, Lin Noueihed, "Jailed Saddam Meets Lawyer," December 17, 2004.

USA Today, Al Arabiya RV via Associated Press, "Saddam's Daughters Express Love for Dad," August 1, 2003.

The National Archives Learning Curve, www.spartacus.schoolnet.co.uk/IRQsaddam: "Saddam Hussein," and pieces by David Hirst, *The Guardian*, December 30, 2006; *The Daily Telegraph*, January 1, 2007; United Press International, December 29, 2006; Am Johal, "The Aesthetics of Execution," AlterNet, January 3, 2007; Robert Scheer, "Saddam: A Monster of Our Creation," Truth Dig, January 3, 2007.

NPR, Lourdes Garcia-Navarro, "Mixed Baghdad Neighborhoods Become Enclaves," November 8, 2008.

Yahoo!News, Mariam Fam, "Saddam Says Shiites Plotted to Kill Him," April 5, 2006.

Yahoo!News, Michael Breen, "The Debt We Owe Iraqi Interpreters," December 9. 2008.

Wikipedia

Al-Faw Palace, last modified May 20, 2009.

Raghad Hussein, last modified March 31, 2009.

Camp Victory: The primary component of the Victory Base Complex, which occupies the area surrounding the Baghdad International Airport. Last modified on February 12, 2009.

Uday Saddam Hussein al-Tikriti, last modified August 20, 2008.

Pruitt-Igoe, last modified June 13, 2009.

Minoru Yamasaki, last modified January 21, 2009.

World News, Associated Press, "Sunni, Shiite Factions Carve Up Baghdad," September 1, 2006.

MISCELLANEOUS

"Why They Built Pruitt-Igoe," excerpted from working paper by Alexander von Hoffman, urban historian, Joint Center for Housing Studies, Harvard University.

NEWSPAPERS

Stars and Stripes, "Car Bombs kill 21 at U.S.-Iraq HG gates," October 5, 2004, 3–5.

New York Times, "Hussein Accuses U.S. Guards of Torture," December 22, 2005.

St. Louis Post-Dispatch, "Saddam trial is postponed again amid disagreement on chief judge," (includes references to Ramsey Clark who says the trial should be abandoned) Hamza Hendawi and Qassim Abdul-Zahra of the Associated Press, January 25, 2006.

St. Louis Post-Dispatch, "Saddam Hussein's trial is adjourned yet another week," Nancy A.

Youssef, Knight Ridder Newspapers, November 29, 2005.

St. Louis Post-Dispatch, "Saddam Hanged; A Legacy of Division," Sabrina Tavernise, *New York Times*, December 31, 2006.

St. Louis Post-Dispatch, "Area Nurse Tended Saddam," Marianna Riley and Aisha Sultan, December 31, 2006.

St. Louis Post-Dispatch, "80 Iraqis Die; Deadliest Month of '06 for U.S.," Lauren Frayer, Associated Press, December 31, 2006.

ACKNOWLEDGMENTS

I WOULD LIKE TO THANK ALL THOSE WHO CONTRIBUTED TO THIS book. First and foremost, I would like to thank my co-conspirator, Marianna Riley, who like me had never written a book but through hard work, passion, and hours of research helped me make this project come true. *Caring for Victor* is my story, but it is our book.

In the course of both living through and writing about the events in this book, I have benefited from the knowledge, advice, support, and camaraderie of many, including Dr. Igor Brondz, who started the ball rolling and who has remained a steadfast and engaged supporter; Dr. Marshall Poger (a.k.a. "the Godfather"), who has been our first reader and consultant who kept us focused and looking for details; Lieutenant Colonel Wayne Sylvester and Sergeant Major Ron Adams, who gave freely, graciously, and generously of their time and knowledge; Sergeant Major Kenneth "True Story" Carpenter, who was by my side from start to finish offering good advice and providing insight and wisdom through every situation; Staff Sergeant Gregory Seavey, who provided information I could not have obtained from any other source; and also Renee Seavey, whose kindness during my dark days of 2004 I will never forget.

FBI Special Agent George Piro is such an integral part of the story that to say we couldn't have done it without him is a gross understatement. He gave generously of his valuable time and shared information we wouldn't have had otherwise and he will always be my friend. We also thank Katherine Schweit, public information officer at the FBI, for facilitating and coordinating it all.

Among the people who have provided encouragement along the way are Dr. Ellis Taylor, Dr. Stefan Craig, Nancy Sanders, Christine Lewis, and Phillip Washington.

Finally, to my wife, Rita, whose loyalty and unwavering support I will never forget—I love you very much.

—Robert Ellis

W E OWE MANY THANKS TO JOSH STEVENS AND MATT HEIDENRY at Reedy Press for immediately seeing the value of our project and never wavering from their commitment to see it through. Their professionalism has made this entire process a pleasurable one.

I, too, am grateful to Wayne Sylvester, Kenneth Carpenter, Ron Adams, and George Piro for their time and knowledge. Not only did they corroborate everything Robert had told me, they provided additional anecdotes and insights that greatly enriched the book.

For their interest—and with our hopes and best wishes for their success—we thank writer, director, and producer Teresa Smith and Alexander Ross of rossWWmedia, who want to make a movie based on our book. We also appreciate the interest of documentary filmmaker and producer Inigo Gilmore.

In addition, we owe thanks for tech support to Virgil Tipton, Elliot Poger, and the patient and professional Celeste Burke.

For their support, interest, and help along the way, we would like to acknowledge Ron Harris, the story's original champion at the *Post-Dispatch*; *Post-Dispatch* editors Ellen Futterman and Susan Hegger, who saw the merit of the story; JillEllyn Riley, Suzanne Topham, and Sanford Poger, who have provided welcome professional advice; Nan Riley, an enthusiastic supporter; and many other cheerleaders, including Beverly Anderson, Patrick Welch, Pamela and Fritz Schaeffer, Robert Duffy, Judy Travelstead, Rosalyn Staadeker, and a host of others who have encouraged us to refrain from procrastination and keep our noses to the grindstone. You know who you are.

And last, but not least, I want to say what an absolute joy it has been to work with Robert Ellis, one of the finest human beings I have ever known. I can't think of how a collaboration could go any more smoothly than ours, and helping him tell his story has—and always will be—one of my fondest achievements.

—Marianna Riley

INDEX

25th Mobile Army Surgical Hospital/ MASH, 13, 45

86th Combat Support Hospital, 166

109th Medical Company, 21–22

10th Mountain Division, 170

112th Military Police, 25, 128, 153

118th Medical Brigade, 27–28, 30, 52, 71, 129, 157-158, 168

301st Combat Support Hospital, 13, 45

439th Military Police Detachment, 15, 21, 27, 66, 84, 87, 112, 155, 157, 167–168, 175

    439th Building, 21, 157

    Courtroom, 112

744th Military Police Battalion, 22

Abu Abbas, Muhammed, 51–53

Abu Ghraib Prison, 65–66, 103, 152, 159

Achille Lauro, 51

Adams, Master Sergeant Ron, 8–9, 11, 15, 58–60, 67, 70, 74–76, 108, 110–111, 114, 123–126, 144, 166, 155, 157, 166, 168, 177

Aerial Port of Debarkation, see APOD.

Air Force, U.S., 53, 168

Ammash, Huda (Mrs. Anthrax, Chemical Sally) 104–111

Al-Bakr, Ahmed Hassan, president of Iraq preceding Saddam Hussein, 131

Al-Faw Palace, 113–114

Al-Jabbouri al-Tai, Sultan Hashem Ahmed, 61

Al Jazeera, 5

Al-Majid, Ali Hassan ("Chemical Ali"/ the King of Spades) 56–58, 62, 94, 124–125

Al-Sadr Brigade, 101–102

Al-Sadr, Muqtada, 101

Al Qaeda, 134

APOD, (Aerial Port of Debarkation), 20, 53, 83, 85, 136, 158, 169

Arab Culture/Customs, 84

Aziz, Tariq 74–76

    And Lawyer, 107

Ba'ath Party, 3, 56, 109, 131–132, 151

Bazaar, 112, 114–116

Baghdad, 1, 3–4, 7–8, 17–21, 24, 26–27, 46, 51, 59, 100, 109, 144, 151, 157–161, 170, 172

Baghdad International Airport (BIAP), 26

Baghdad University, 109

Balad, 161

Beheadings, 31, 60, 96–97, 99

Berg, Nick, 98

Bin Laden, Osama, 134

Bird Man of Alcatraz, 70

Blackwater USA Bridge, 152

Blix, Hans, 110

Bogota, Columbia, 5

Bremer, Paul, 63

Brondz, Igor, M.D., 2–4

Bulgaria, 5

Bush, President George W., 13, 51, 84

Camp Cropper, 1, 3–4, 22–23, 26–27, 31–32, 46–47, 50–69, 86–87, 89, 91, 94–96, 99, 104, 107, 112–113, 116, 118, 123–124, 128, 131, 141, 146, 148, 152–153, 155–157, 165

Camp Cropper clinic, 21, 25, 27, 30–31, 52–55, 65–66, 68, 72, 77, 104, 127, 152–153

Camp Udairi, 7, 16

Camp Victory, 26–27, 112, 123–124, 148, 168

Camp Wolverine, 140

Carpenter, Sergeant Major Kenneth (True Story), 8–9, 15, 22, 63, 67, 84, 108, 123, 139, 142, 146, 149, 168

Carr Square Village, 34

Carr Lane Elementary School, 35

CPR, 52–53

Chemical Ali, see Al-Majid, Ali Hassan.

Cheney, Vice President Richard 16

Clark, Ramsey, 166
Cohen, Specialist Nathan, 8, 15
Combat Support Hospital/CSH, 27, 55,
    83–88, 99, 100, 102–103, 129–130,
    157–158, 160–162, 164–166, 168
Contractors, 27, 127, 144, 152, 155–156,
    160, 166
Cropper Doc, 89, 91, 95, 107, 116, 118,
    141, 146
Darst, Joseph M. (St. Louis mayor), 34
Deavault, Dorothy 38, 41, 141, 143
Depleted Uranium, 109
Delta Company, 87, 155, 165
Desert Storm, 13, 109, 133
Dishdasha, 24, 73, 78, 171–172
Downs, David, 40
Downs, Michael, 40
Duelfer, Charles, 32
Drew, Hank, 40
Ehler, Sergeant First Class Randy, 8, 15
Ellis, Larry, 37, 40, 135, 140–141, 143
Ellis, Rita French 13–14, 32–33, 41, 89–90,
    101, 115–116, 135, 143, 170
Fallujah, 25, 151–153
Flak jackets, 10, 14
    Lack of armor, 10
Fort Dodge, 14
Fort Omaha, 14
Fort Riley, 14, 84, 170
Foster, Lola (Robert's Mother), 32–33, 39,
    43–44
Foster, Norma, 45
Franklin, Charles, 39
Gater Necks, 12
Geneva Conventions, 73
Goering, Hermann, 46
Green Zone, 99, 157–160
Gulf War, see Desert Storm.
Hadji shop, 96, 98
Hall, Sharon, 40–41
Hasan al-Tikriti, Barzan Ibrahim, 59–60, 75
Hussein, Hala, 93
Hussein, Qusay, 61, 92–93
Hussein, Raghad, 93–95
Hussein, Rana, 93–95
Hussein, Sabha, 172
Hussein, Saddam
    abdominal pain, 81–88

administration, 132–133
Al Qaeda, 134
arraignment, 157
birds, 70
cigars, 96, 112–114, 11–118, 135, 141
crying, 131
CT scan, 83, 85–86
execution, 177–178
eye glasses, 120
family, 92–95
first meeting, 23–24
health, 25, 29, 31, 50, 79, 112, 117, 147
hunger strike, 47–49
"garden," 70–71, 141
language, 68–69
poetry, 90–91, 147–148
trial, 122–123
watch (time), 118–119
wet wipes, 71–72
writing, 29, 118, 120, 130, 133
Hussein, Sajida Khairallah Tulfah, 93
Hussein, Samira Shahbandar, 93
Hussein, Sabha, 172
Hussein, Uday, 92–94, 144–145, 149
Haliburton Company, 16
Hesco Barriers, 19–20, 71, 77
High-Value Detainees (HVDs) 6, 23, 26,
    54, 56
Igoe, William L., 37
International Committee of the Red Cross,
    (ICRC), 33, 63, 65–67, 123, 135–136,
    139
Interim Iraqi government, 62, 66, 122–123
Interrogation Trailers, 8–9, 21, 32
Interrogations, 31–32, 48–49, 54, 92, 118
Iran, 56–57, 120, 132, 148
Iran-Iraq War, 57, 61
Iraqi contractors, see Contractors.
Iraqi Freedom, 13
Iraqi Most Wanted Playing Cards, 4–5, 51,
    61, 64, 74, 82
Iraqi Survey Group, 32
Iraqi Tribunal, 148
Irinaga, Todd, 28
Israel, 119–120
Jayhawker 6, see Sylvester, Lieutenant
    Colonel Wayne.
Judaism, 119

Kamel, Hussein, 95
Kamel, Saddam, 95
Kansas, University of, 111
Keystone Cops, 15
Kuwaiti Desert, 7, 16, 18
Kuwait, 8, 16, 56, 132–133, 139–140, 144, 154, 169
Kurds, 56–57, 61, 171
Khulenengel, Major Mark, 15
Klinghoffer, Leon, 51
Meals Ready to eat (MRE), 47, 75–76
Missouri, University of, 110–111
Mississippi River, 138
Mumbly Peg, 137–138
Napier, Sergeant Major Ronald, 8
North Victory, 112, 123–124, 168
Nuremberg trials, 46
Operation Hotel Victor, 83–84
Page, Sergeant John, 11, 15
Palestine Liberation Front, 51
Palestine National Authority, 51
Peeples, Larry, 40
Peeples, Marvin, 40
Peeples, Troy, 40
Persians, 120
Peterson, Staff Sergeant Loren, 8, 15
Phantom Fury, 152
Piro, George, 1–2, 5, 28–30, 48–49, 66, 69–71, 73, 78, 82, 84, 91–92, 95, 118, 131, 146, 174, 178
Pope, Beverly 36, 90
Pope, Lionel, 90
Post-Exchange (PX), 114–115, 140, 169
Porta Johns, 116, 127
    And hand grenades, 128
Pruitt-Igoe, 34–45, 137
Pruitt, Wendell Oliver, 37
Quran, 84, 119
Ramadan, 58, 75, 100
Reagan, Ronald, U.S. President, 148
Red Cross, see International Committee of the Red Cross.
Rumsfeld, Donald, Secretary of Defense,
10, 162
Rogers, Melvin, 39
Route Irish, 99, 101–102, 129–130, 158
Route Tampa, 101, 158
Sadr City, 59, 101, 158
Schwarzkopf, Norman, 61
Seavey, Sergeant Gregory, 11, 15, 122–123, 126
Special Weapons & Tactics (SWAT) Training, 14
St. Joseph Health Center, 2
St. Louis Housing Authority, 43
St. Louis Lambert International Airport, 36
St. Louis Post-Dispatch, 5, 34, 177
Sun, The, 73
Sylvester, Lieutenant Colonel Wayne (Jayhawker 6), 8, 15, 24, 27, 31, 47–48, 55, 66–67, 73, 75, 88, 102, 106, 108–110, 123–125, 136, 147, 166
Tactical Operations Center/TOC, 83, 139, 165
Tawina, Na'im, 119–120
Texas Women's University, 108
Tiger Teams, 60–61
Tikrit, 172
True Story, see Carpenter, Sergeant Major Kenneth.
Tuzzio, Sergeant Jeremiah, 8, 15
Uday's Palace, 144–145, 149
Uniform Code of Military Justice, 73
United Nations Special Commission (UNSCOM), 95, 151
Vehicle-borne improvised explosive device (VBIED), 130
Victor, see Hussein, Saddam.
Washington, Phillip, 39
Weapons of Mass Destruction (WMD), 58, 110, 148
Williams, Ernest, 40
Wilkins, Doc, 169–170, 176
Wood, The, 21–23, 28, 53, 76–77, 81, 88, 120, 168
World Trade Center, 36, 44
Yamasaki, Minoru, 36–37, 44
Zionists, 120